Green Fields and Running Brooks & Other Poems by James Whitcomb Riley

Poet and author James Whitcomb Riley was born on October 7th 1849 in Greenfield, Indiana. Better known as the "Hoosier Poet" for his work with regional dialects, and also as the "Children's Poet" Riley was born into an influential and well off family.

However his education was spotty but he was surrounded by creativity which was to stand him in good stead later in life.

His early career was a series of low paid temporary jobs. After stints as a journalist and billboard proprietor he had the resources to dedicate more of his efforts to writing.

Riley was prone to drink which was to affect his health and later his career but after a slow start and a lot of submissions he began to gain traction first in newspapers and then with the publication of his dialect poems 'Boone County Poems' he came to national recognition. This propelled him to long term contracts to perform on speaking circuits. These were very successful but over the years his star waned.

In 1888 he was too drunk to perform and the ensuing publicity made everything seem very bleak for a while. However he overcame that and managed to re-negotiate his contracts so that he received his rightful share of the income and his wealth thereafter increased very quickly.

A bachelor, Riley seems to have his writings as his only outlet, and although in his public performances he was well received, his publications were becoming seen as banal and repetitive and sales of these later works began to fall away.

Eventually after his last tour in 1895 he retired to spend his final years in Indianapolis writing patriotic poetry.

Now in poor health, weakened by years of heavy drinking, Riley, the Hoosier Poet died on July 23, 1916 of a stroke. In a final, unusual tribute, Riley lay in state for a day in the Indiana Statehouse, where thousands came to pay their respects. Not since Lincoln had a public personage received such a send-off. He is buried at Crown Hill Cemetery in Indianapolis.

Index Of Poems
GREEN FIELDS AND RUNNING BROOKS
A COUNTRY PATHWAY
ON THE BANKS O' DEER CRICK
A DITTY OF NO TONE.
A WATER-COLOR
THE CYCLONE
WHERE-AWAY
THE HOME-GOING
HOW JOHN QUIT THE FARM.
NORTH AND SOUTH
THE IRON HORSE

HIS MOTHER'S WAY
JAP MILLER
A SOUTHERN SINGER
A DREAM OF AUTUMN.
TOM VAN ARDEN
JUST TO BE GOOD
HOME AT NIGHT
THE HOOSIER FOLK-CHILD
JACK THE GIANT KILLER
WHILE THE MUSICIAN PLAYED.
AUGUST
TO HEAR HER SING
BEING HIS MOTHER
JUNE AT WOODRUFF.
FARMER WHIPPLE - BACHELOR.
DAWN, NOON AND DEWFALL
NESSMUK
AS MY UNCLE USED TO SAY
THE SINGER
A FULL HARVEST
BLIND
RIGHT HERE AT HOME
THE LITTLE FAT DOCTOR
THE SHOEMAKER
THE OLD RETIRED SEA CAPTAIN
ROBERT BURNS WILSON
TO THE SERENADER
THE WIFE-BLESSÉD
SISTER JONES'S CONFESSION
THE CURSE OF THE WANDERING FOOT
A MONUMENT FOR THE SOLDIERS
THE RIVAL
IRY AND BILLY AND JO
A WRAITH OF SUMMERTIME
HER BEAUTIFUL EYES
DOT LEEDLE BOY
DONN PIATT OF MAC-O-CHEE
THEM FLOWERS
THE QUIET LODGER
THE WATCHES OF THE NIGHT
HIS VIGIL
THE PLAINT HUMAN
BY ANY OTHER NAME
TO AN IMPORTUNATE GHOST
THE QUARREL
THE OLD YEAR AND THE NEW
THE HEREAFTER
JOHN BROWN
A CUP OF TEA
JUDITH
THE ARTEMUS OF MICHIGAN

THE HOODOO
THE RIVALS; OR THE SHOWMAN'S RUSE
WHAT CHRIS'MAS FETCHED THE WIGGINSES
GO, WINTER!
ELIZABETH
SLEEP
DAN PAINE
OLD WINTERS ON THE FARM
AT UTTER LOAF.
A LOUNGER
A SONG OF LONG AGO
THE CHANT OF THE CROSS-BEARING CHILD
THANKSGIVING
AUTUMN
THE TWINS
BEDOUIN
TUGG MARTIN.
LET US FORGET
JOHN ALDEN AND PERCILLY
REACH YOUR HAND TO ME
THE ROSE
MY FRIEND
SUSPENSE
THE PASSING OF A HEART
BY HER WHITE BED
WE TO SIGH INSTEAD OF SING
THE BLOSSOMS ON THE TREES
A DISCOURAGING MODEL
LAST NIGHT - AND THIS
SEPTEMBER DARK
A GLIMPSE OF PAN
OUT OF NAZARETH
THE WANDERING JEW
LONGFELLOW
JOHN MCKEEN
THEIR SWEET SORROW
SOME SCATTERING REMARKS OF BUB'S
MR. WHAT'S-HIS-NAME
WHEN AGE COMES ON
ENVOY

James Whitcomb Riley – A Short Biography

GREEN FIELDS AND RUNNING BROOKS
Ho! green fields and running brooks!
Knotted strings and fishing-hooks
Of the truant, stealing down
Weedy backways of the town.

Where the sunshine overlooks,
By green fields and running brooks,
All intruding guests of chance
With a golden tolerance,

Cooing doves, or pensive pair
Of picnickers, straying there
By green fields and running brooks,
Sylvan shades and mossy nooks!

And O Dreamer of the Days,
Murmurer of roundelays
All unsung of words or books,
Sing green fields and running brooks!

A COUNTRY PATHWAY

I come upon it suddenly, alone
A little pathway winding in the weeds
That fringe the roadside; and with dreams my own,
I wander as it leads.

Full wistfully along the slender way,
Through summer tan of freckled shade and shine,
I take the path that leads me as it may
Its every choice is mine.

A chipmunk, or a sudden-whirring quail,
Is startled by my step as on I fare
A garter-snake across the dusty trail
Glances and is not there.

Above the arching jimson-weeds flare twos
And twos of sallow-yellow butterflies,
Like blooms of lorn primroses blowing loose
When autumn winds arise.

The trail dips, dwindles, broadens then, and lifts
Itself astride a cross-road dubiously,
And, from the fennel marge beyond it, drifts
Still onward, beckoning me.

And though it needs must lure me mile on mile
Out of the public highway, still I go,
My thoughts, far in advance in Indian-file,
Allure me even so.

Why, I am as a long-lost boy that went
At dusk to bring the cattle to the bars,
And was not found again, though Heaven lent

His mother ail the stars

With which to seek him through that awful night.
O years of nights as vain! Stars never rise
But well might miss their glitter in the light
Of tears in mother-eyes!

So on, with quickened breaths, I follow still
My avant-courier must be obeyed!
Thus am I led, and thus the path, at will,
Invites me to invade

A meadow's precincts, where my daring guide
Clambers the steps of an old-fashioned stile,
And stumbles down again, the other side,
To gambol there awhile

In pranks of hide-and-seek, as on ahead
I see it running, while the clover-stalks
Shake rosy fists at me, as though they said
"You dog our country-walks

And mutilate us with your walking-stick!
We will not suffer tamely what you do
And warn you at your peril, for we'll sic
Our bumble-bees on you!"

But I smile back, in airy nonchalance,
The more determined on my wayward quest,
As some bright memory a moment dawns
A morning in my breast

Sending a thrill that hurries me along
In faulty similes of childish skips,
Enthused with lithe contortions of a song
Performing on my lips.

In wild meanderings o'er pasture wealth
Erratic wanderings through dead'ning-lands,
Where sly old brambles, plucking me by stealth,
Put berries in my hands:

Or, the path climbs a boulder, wades a slough
Or, rollicking through buttercups and flags,
Goes gaily dancing o'er a deep bayou
On old tree-trunks and snags:

Or, at the creek, leads o'er a limpid pool
Upon a bridge the stream itself has made,
With some Spring-freshet for the mighty tool
That its foundation laid.

I pause a moment here to bend and muse,
With dreamy eyes, on my reflection, where
A boat-backed bug drifts on a helpless cruise,
Or wildly oars the air,

As, dimly seen, the pirate of the brook
The pike, whose jaunty hulk denotes his speed
Swings pivoting about, with wary look
Of low and cunning greed.

Till, filled with other thought, I turn again
To where the pathway enters in a realm
Of lordly woodland, under sovereign reign
Of towering oak and elm.

A puritanic quiet here reviles
The almost whispered warble from the hedge,
And takes a locust's rasping voice and files
The silence to an edge.

In such a solitude my somber way
Strays like a misanthrope within a gloom
Of his own shadows till the perfect day
Bursts into sudden bloom,

And crowns a long, declining stretch of space,
Where King Corn's armies lie with flags unfurled,
And where the valley's dint in Nature's face
Dimples a smiling world.

And lo! through mists that may not be dispelled,
I see an old farm homestead, as in dreams,
Where, like a gem in costly setting held,
The old log cabin gleams.

O darling Pathway! lead me bravely on
Adown your valley way, and run before
Among the roses crowding up the lawn
And thronging at the door,

And carry up the echo there that shall
Arouse the drowsy dog, that he may bay
The household out to greet the prodigal
That wanders home to-day.

ON THE BANKS O' DEER CRICK

On the banks o' Deer Crick! There's the place fer me!
Worter slidin' past ye jes as clair as it kin be:

See yer shadder in it, and the shadder o' the sky,
And the shadder o' the buzzard as he goes a-lazein' by;
Shadder o' the pizen-vines, and shadder o' the trees
And I purt'-nigh said the shadder o' the sunshine and the breeze!
Well I never seen the ocean ner I never seen the sea:
On the banks o' Deer Crick's grand enough fer me!

On the banks o' Deer Crick mild er two from town
'Long up where the mill-race comes a-loafin' down,
Like to git up in there 'mongst the sycamores
And watch the worter at the dam, a-frothin' as she pours:
Crawl out on some old log, with my hook and line,
Where the fish is jes so thick you kin see 'em shine
As they flicker round yer bait, coaxin' you to jerk,
Tel yer tired ketchin' of 'em, mighty nigh, as work!

On the banks o' Deer Crick! Allus my delight
Jes to be around there take it day er night!
Watch the snipes and killdees foolin' half the day
Er these-'ere little worter-bugs skootin' ever'way!
Snakefeeders glancin' round, er dartin' out o' sight;
And dew-fall, and bullfrogs, and lightnin'-bugs at night
Stars up through the tree-tops, er in the crick below,
And smell o' mussrat through the dark clean from the old b'y-o!

Er take a tromp, some Sund'y, say, 'way up to "Johnson's Hole,"
And find where he's had a fire, and hid his fishin' pole;
Have yer "dog-leg," with ye and yer pipe and "cut-and-dry"
Pocketful o' corn-bred, and slug er two o' rye,
Soak yer hide in sunshine and waller in the shade
Like the Good Book tells us, "where there're none to make afraid!"
Well! I never seen the ocean ner I never seen the sea
On the banks o' Deer Crick's grand enough fer me!

A DITTY OF NO TONE.
Piped to the Spirit of John Keats.

I.
Would that my lips might pour out in thy praise
A fitting melody, an air sublime,
A song sun-washed and draped in dreamy haze
The floss and velvet of luxurious rhyme:
A lay wrought of warm languors, and o'er-brimmed
With balminess, and fragrance of wild flowers
Such as the droning bee ne'er wearies of
Such thoughts as might be hymned
To thee from this midsummer land of ours
Through shower and sunshine blent for very love.

II.
Deep silences in woody aisles where through
Cool paths go loitering, and where the trill
Of best-remembered birds hath something new
In cadence for the hearing lingering still
Through all the open day that lies beyond;
Reaches of pasture-lands, vine-wreathen oaks,
Majestic still in pathos of decay,
The road, the wayside pond
Wherein the dragonfly an instant soaks
His filmy wing-tips ere he flits away.

III.
And I would pluck from out the dank, rich mould,
Thick-shaded from the sun of noon, the long
Lithe stalks of barley, topped with ruddy gold,
And braid them in the meshes of my song;
And with them I would tangle wheat and rye,
And wisps of greenest grass the katydid
Ere crept beneath the blades of, sulkily,
As harvest-hands went by;
And weave of all, as wildest fancy bid,
A crown of mingled song and bloom for thee.

A WATER-COLOR
Low hidden in among the forest trees
An artist's tilted easel, ankle-deep
In tousled ferns and mosses, and in these
A fluffy water-spaniel, half asleep
Beside a sketch-book and a fallen hat
A little wicker flask tossed into that.

A sense of utter carelessness and grace
Of pure abandon in the slumb'rous scene,
As if the June, all hoydenish of face,
Had romped herself to sleep there on the green,
And brink and sagging bridge and sliding stream
Were just romantic parcels of her dream.

THE CYCLONE
So lone I stood, the very trees seemed drawn
In conference with themselves. Intense intense
Seemed everything; he summer splendor on
The sight, magnificence!

A babe's life might not lighter fail and die
Than failed the sunlight. Though the hour was noon,

The palm of midnight might not lighter lie
Upon the brow of June.

With eyes upraised, I saw the underwings
Of swallows, gone the instant afterward
While from the elms there came strange twitterings,
Stilled scarce ere they were heard.

The river seemed to shiver; and, far down
Its darkened length, I saw the sycamores
Lean inward closer, under the vast frown
That weighed above the shores.

Then was a roar, born of some awful burst!
And one lay, shrieking, chattering, in my path
Flung, he or I, out of some space accurst
As of Jehovah's wrath:

Nor barely had he wreaked his latest prayer,
Ere back the noon flashed o'er the ruin done,
And, o'er uprooted forests touseled there,
The birds sang in the sun.

WHERE-AWAY

O the Lands of Where-Away!
Tell us, tell us, where are they?
Through the darkness and the dawn
We have journeyed on and on
From the cradle to the cross
From possession unto loss,
Seeking still, from day to day,
For the lands of Where-Away.

When our baby-feet were first
Planted where the daisies burst,
And the greenest grasses grew
In the fields we wandered through,
On, with childish discontent,
Ever on and on we went,
Hoping still to pass, some day,
O'er the verge of Where-Away.

Roses laid their velvet lips
On our own, with fragrant sips;
But their kisses held us not,
All their sweetness we forgot;
Though the brambles in our track
Plucked at us to hold us back
"Just ahead," we used to say,

"Lie the Lands of Where-Away."

Children at the pasture-bars,
Through the dusk, like glimmering stars,
Waved their hands that we should bide
With them over eventide:
Down the dark their voices failed
Falteringly, as they hailed,
And died into yesterday
Night ahead and - Where-Away?

Twining arms about us thrown
Warm caresses, all our own,
Can but stay us for a spell
Love hath little new to tell
To the soul in need supreme,
Aching ever with the dream
Of the endless bliss it may
Find in Lands of Where-Away!

THE HOME-GOING

We must get home for we have been away
So long it seems forever and a day!
And O so very homesick we have grown,
The laughter of the world is like a moan
In our tired hearing, and its songs as vain,
We must get home, we must get home again!

We must get home: It hurts so, staying here,
Where fond hearts must be wept out tear by tear,
And where to wear wet lashes means, at best,
When most our lack, the least our hope of rest
When most our need of joy, the more our pain
We must get home, we must get home again!

We must get home: All is so quiet there:
The touch of loving hands on brow and hair
Dim rooms, wherein the sunshine is made mild -
The lost love of the mother and the child
Restored in restful lullabies of rain.
We must get home, we must get home again!

We must get home, where, as we nod and drowse,
Time humors us and tiptoes through the house,
And loves us best when sleeping baby-wise,
With dreams, not tear-drops, brimming our clenched eyes,
Pure dreams that know nor taint nor earthly stain
We must get home, we must get home again!

We must get home; and, unremembering there
All gain of all ambitions otherwhere,
Rest from the feverish victory, and the crown
Of conquest whose waste glory weighs us down.
Fame's fairest gifts we toss back with disdain
We must get home, we must get home again!

HOW JOHN QUIT THE FARM.

Nobody on the old farm here but Mother, me and John,
Except, of course, the extry he'p when harvest-time come on
And then, I want to say to you, we needed he'p about,
As you'd admit, ef you'd a-seen the way the crops turned out!

A better quarter-section, ner a richer soil warn't found
Than this-here old-home place o' ourn fer fifty miles around!
The house was small but plenty-big we found it from the day
That John, our only livin' son, packed up and went way.

You see, we tuck sich pride in John, his mother more 'n me
That's natchurul; but both of us was proud as proud could be;
Fer the boy, from a little chap, was most oncommon bright,
And seemed in work as well as play to take the same delight.

He allus went a-whistlin' round the place, as glad at heart
As robins up at five o'clock to git an airly start;
And many a time 'fore daylight Mother's waked me up to say
"Jest listen, David! listen! Johnny's beat the birds to-day!"

High-sperited from boyhood, with a most inquirin' turn,
He wanted to learn ever'thing on earth they was to learn:
He'd ast more plaguey questions in a mortal-minute here
Than his grandpap in Paradise could answer in a year!

And read! w'y, his own mother learnt him how to read and spell;
And "The Childern of the Abbey" w'y, he knowed that book as well
At fifteen as his parents! and "The Pilgrim's Progress," too
Jest knuckled down, the shaver did, and read 'em through and through!

At eighteen, Mother 'lowed the boy must have a better chance
That we ort to educate him, under any circumstance;
And John he j'ined his mother, and they ding-donged and kep' on,
Tel I sent him off to school in town, half glad that he was gone.

But, I missed him, w'y of course I did! The Fall and Winter through
I never built the kitchen-fire, er split a stick in two,
Er fed the stock, er butchered, er swung up a gambrel-pin,
But what I thought o' John, and wished that he was home agin.

He'd come, sometimes, on Sund'ys most, and stay the Sund'y out;

And on Thanksgivin'-Day he 'peared to like to be about:
But a change was workin' on him, he was stiller than before,
And did n't joke, ner laugh, ner sing and whistle any more.

And his talk was all so proper; and I noticed, with a sigh,
He was tryin' to raise side-whiskers, and had on a striped tie,
And a standin'-collar, ironed up as stiff and slick as bone;
And a breast-pin, and a watch and chain and plug-hat of his own.

But when Spring-weather opened out, and John was to come home
And he'p me through the season, I was glad to see him come;
But my happiness, that evening, with the settin' sun went down,
When he bragged of "a position" that was offered him in town.

"But," says I, "you'll not accept it?" "W'y, of course
I will," says he.
"This drudgin' on a farm," he says, "is not the life fer me;
I've set my stakes up higher," he continued, light and gay,
"And town's the place fer me, and I'm a-goin' right away!"

And go he did! his mother clingin' to him at the gate,
A-pleadin' and a-cryin'; but it hadn't any weight.
I was tranquiller, and told her 'twarn't no use to worry so,
And onclasped her arms from round his neck round mine and let him go!

I felt a little bitter feelin' foolin' round about
The aidges of my conscience; but I didn't let it out;
I simply retch out, trimbly-like, and tuck the boy's hand,
And though I did n't say a word, I knowed he'd understand.

And well! sence then the old home here was mighty lonesome, shore!
With me a-workin' in the field, and Mother at the door,
Her face ferever to'rds the town, and fadin' more and more
Her only son nine miles away, a-clerkin' in a store!

The weeks and months dragged by us; and sometimes the boy would write
A letter to his mother, savin' that his work was light,
And not to feel oneasy about his health a bit
Though his business was confinin', he was gittin' used to it.

And sometimes he would write and ast how I was gittin' on,
And ef I had to pay out much fer he'p sence he was gone;
And how the hogs was doin', and the balance of the stock,
And talk on fer a page er two jest like he used to talk.

And he wrote, along 'fore harvest, that he guessed he would git home,
Fer business would, of course be dull in town. But didn't come:
We got a postal later, sayin' when they had no trade
They filled the time "invoicin' goods," and that was why he staid.

And then he quit a-writin' altogether: Not a word

Exceptin' what the neighbors brung who'd been to town and heard
What store John was clerkin' in, and went round to inquire
If they could buy their goods there less and sell their produce higher.

And so the Summer faded out, and Autumn wore away,
And a keener Winter never fetched around Thanksgivin'-Day!
The night before that day of thanks I'll never quite fergit,
The wind a-howlin' round the house, it makes me creepy yit!

And there set me and Mother, me a-twistin' at the prongs
Of a green scrub-ellum forestick with a vicious pair of tongs,
And Mother sayin', "David! David!" in a' undertone,
As though she thought that I was thinkin' bad-words unbeknown.

"I've dressed the turkey, David, fer to-morrow," Mother said,
A-tryin' to wedge some pleasant subject in my stubborn head,
"And the mince-meat I'm a-mixin' is perfection mighty nigh;
And the pound-cake is delicious-rich " - "Who'll eat 'em?" I-says-I.

"The cramberries is drippin-sweet," says Mother, runnin' on,
P'tendin' not to hear me; "and somehow I thought of John
All the time they was a-jellin' fer you know they allus was
His favour he likes 'em so!" Says I, "Well, s'pose he does?"

"Oh, nothin' much!" says Mother, with a quiet sort o' smile
"This gentleman behind my cheer may tell you after while!"
And as I turned and looked around, some one riz up and leant
And put his arms round Mother's neck, and laughed in low content.

"It's me," he says "your fool-boy John, come back to shake your hand;
Set down with you, and talk with you, and make you understand
How dearer yit than all the world is this old home that we
Will spend Thanksgivin' in fer life, jest Mother, you and me!"

Nobody on the old farm here but Mother, me and John,
Except of course the extry he'p, when harvest-time comes on;
And then, I want to say to you, we need sich he'p about,
As you'd admit, ef you could see the way the crops turns out!

NORTH AND SOUTH
Of the North I wove a dream,
All bespangled with the gleam
Of the glancing wings of swallows
Dipping ripples in a stream,
That, like a tide of wine,
Wound through lands of shade and shine
Where purple grapes hung bursting on the vine.

And where orchard-boughs were bent

Till their tawny fruitage blent
With the golden wake that marked the
Way the happy reapers went;
Where the dawn died into noon
As the May-mists into June,
And the dusk fell like a sweet face in a swoon.

Of the South I dreamed: And there
Came a vision clear and fair
As the marvelous enchantments
Of the mirage of the air;
And I saw the bayou-trees,
With their lavish draperies,
Hang heavy o'er the moon-washed cypress-knees.

Peering from lush fens of rice,
I beheld the Negro's eyes,
Lit with that old superstition
Death itself can not disguise;
And I saw the palm tree nod
Like an oriental god,
And the cotton froth and bubble from the pod,

And I dreamed that North and South,
With a sigh of dew and drouth,
Blew each unto the other
The salute of lip and mouth;
And I wakened, awed and thrilled
Every doubting murmur stilled
In the silence of the dream I found fulfilled.

THE IRON HORSE

No song is mine of Arab steed
My courser is of nobler blood,
And cleaner limb and fleeter speed,
And greater strength and hardihood
Than ever cantered wild and free
Across the plains of Araby.

Go search the level desert-land
From Sana on to Samarcand
Wherever Persian prince has been
Or Dervish, Sheik or Bedouin,
And I defy you there to point
Me out a steed the half so fine
From tip of ear to pastern-joint
As this old iron horse of mine.

You do not know what beauty is

You do not know what gentleness
His answer is to my caress!
Why, look upon this gait of his,
A touch upon his iron rein
He moves with such a stately grace
The sunlight on his burnished mane
Is barely shaken in its place;
And at touch he changes pace,
And, gliding backward, stops again.

And talk of mettle - Ah! my friend,
Such passion smoulders in his breast
That when awakened it will send
A thrill of rapture wilder than
Ere palpitated heart of man
When flaming at its mightiest.
And there's a fierceness in his ire
A maddened majesty that leaps
Along his veins in blood of fire,
Until the path his vision sweeps
Spins out behind him like a thread
Unraveled from the reel of time,
As, wheeling on his course sublime,
The earth revolves beneath his tread.

Then stretch away, my gallant steed!
Thy mission is a noble one:
You bear the father to the son,
And sweet relief to bitter need;
You bear the stranger to his friends;
You bear the pilgrim to the shrine,
And back again the prayer he sends
That God will prosper me and mine,
The star that on thy forehead gleams
Has blossomed in our brightest dreams.
Then speed thee on thy glorious race!
The mother waits thy ringing pace;
The father leans an anxious ear
The thunder of thy hoofs to hear;
The lover listens, far away,
To catch thy keen exultant neigh;
And, where thy breathings roll and rise,
The husband strains his eager eyes,
And laugh of wife and baby-glee
Ring out to greet and welcome thee.
Then stretch away! and when at last
The master's hand shall gently check
Thy mighty speed, and hold thee fast,
The world will pat thee on the neck.

HIS MOTHER'S WAY

Tomps 'ud allus haf to say
Somepin' 'bout "his mother's way."
He lived hard-like, never jined
Any church of any kind.
"It was Mother's way," says he,
"To be good enough fer me
And her too, and certinly
Lord has heerd her pray!"
Propped up on his dyin' bed,
"Shore as Heaven's overhead,
I'm a-goin' there," he said
"It was Mother's way."

JAP MILLER

Jap Miller down at Martinsville's the blamedest feller yit!
When he starts in a-talkin' other folks is apt to quit!
'Pears like that mouth o' his'n wuz n't made fer nuthin' else
But jes' to argify 'em down and gether in their pelts:
He'll talk you down on tariff; er he'll talk you down on tax,
And prove the pore man pays 'em all and them's about the fac's!
Religen, law, er politics, prize-fightin', er base-ball
Jes' tetch Jap up a little and he'll post you 'bout 'em all.

And the comicalist feller ever tilted back a cheer
And tuck a chaw tobacker kind o' like he did n't keer.
There's where the feller's strength lays, he's so
common-like and plain,
They haint no dude about old Jap, you bet you, nary grain!
They 'lected him to Council and it never turned his head,
And did n't make no differunce what anybody said,
He didn't dress no finer, ner rag out in fancy clothes;
But his voice in Council-meetin's is a turrer to his foes.

He's fer the pore man ever' time! And in the last campaign
He stumped old Morgan County, through the sunshine and the rain,
And helt the banner up'ards from a-trailin' in the dust,
And cut loose on monopolies and cuss'd and cuss'd and cuss'd!
He'd tell some funny story ever' now and then, you know,
Tel, blame it! it wuz better 'n a jack-o'-lantern show!
And I'd go furder, yit, to-day, to hear old Jap norate
Than any high-toned orator 'at ever stumped the State!

W'y, that-air blame Jap Miller, with his keen sircastic fun,
Has got more friends than ary candidate 'at ever run!
Do n't matter what his views is, when he states the same to you,
They allus coincide with your'n, the same as two and two:
You can't take issue with him, er, at least, they haint no sense

In startin' in to down him, so you better not commence.
The best way's jes' to listen, like your humble servant does,
And jes' concede Jap Miller is the best man ever wuz!

A SOUTHERN SINGER
Written In Madison Caweln's "Lyrics and Idyls."

Herein are blown from out the South
Songs blithe as those of Pan's pursed mouth
As sweet in voice as, in perfume,
The night-breath of magnolia-bloom.

Such sumptuous languor lures the sense
Such luxury of indolence
The eyes blur as a nymph's might blur,
With water-lilies watching her.

You waken, thrilling at the trill
Of some wild bird that seems to spill
The silence full of winey drips
Of song that Fancy sips and sips.

Betimes, in brambled lanes wherethrough
The chipmunk stripes himself from view,
You pause to lop a creamy spray
Of elder-blossoms by the way.

Or where the morning dew is yet
Gray on the topmost rail, you set
A sudden palm and, vaulting, meet
Your vaulting shadow in the wheat.

On lordly swards, of suave incline,
Entessellate with shade and shine,
You shall misdoubt your lowly birth,
Clad on as one of princely worth:

The falcon on your wrist shall ride
Your milk-white Arab side by side
With one of raven-black. You fain
Would kiss the hand that holds the rein.

Nay, nay, Romancer! Poet! Seer!
Sing us back home from there to here;
Grant your high grace and wit, but we
Most honor your simplicity.

Herein are blown from out the South
Songs blithe as those of Pan's pursed mouth

As sweet in voice as, in perfume,
The night-breath of magnolia-bloom.

A DREAM OF AUTUMN.

Mellow hazes, lowly trailing
Over wood and meadow, veiling
Somber skies, with wildfowl sailing
Sailor-like to foreign lands;
And the north-wind overleaping
Summer's brink, and floodlike sweeping
Wrecks of roses where the weeping
Willows wring their helpless hands.

Flared, like Titan torches flinging
Flakes of flame and embers, springing
From the vale the trees stand swinging
In the moaning atmosphere;
While in dead'ning-lands the lowing
Of the cattle, sadder growing,
Fills the sense to overflowing
With the sorrow of the year.

Sorrowfully, yet the sweeter
Sings the brook in rippled meter
Under boughs that lithely teeter
Lorn birds, answering from the shores
Through the viny, shady-shiny
Interspaces, shot with tiny
Flying motes that fleck the winy
Wave-engraven sycamores.

Fields of ragged stubble, wrangled
With rank weeds, and shocks of tangled
Corn, with crests like rent plumes dangled
Over Harvest's battle-piain;
And the sudden whir and whistle
Of the quail that, like a missile,
Whizzes over thorn and thistle,
And, a missile, drops again.

Muffled voices, hid in thickets
Where the redbird stops to stick its
Ruddy beak betwixt the pickets
Of the truant's rustic trap;
And the sound of laughter ringing
Where, within the wild-vine swinging,
Climb Bacchante's schoolmates, flinging
Purple clusters in her lap.

Rich as wine, the sunset flashes
Round the tilted world, and dashes
Up the sloping west and splashes
Red foam over sky and sea
Till my dream of Autumn, paling
In the splendor all-prevailing,
Like a sallow leaf goes sailing
Down the silence solemnly.

TOM VAN ARDEN

Tom Van Arden, my old friend,
Our warm fellowship is one
Far too old to comprehend
Where its bond was first begun:
Mirage-like before my gaze
Gleams a land of other days,
Where two truant boys, astray,
Dream their lazy lives away.

There's a vision, in the guise
Of Midsummer, where the Past
Like a weary beggar lies
In the shadow Time has cast;
And as blends the bloom of trees
With the drowsy hum of bees,
Fragrant thoughts and murmurs blend,
Tom Van Arden, my old friend.

Tom Van Arden, my old friend,
All the pleasures we have known
Thrill me now as I extend
This old hand and grasp your own
Feeling, in the rude caress,
All affection's tenderness;
Feeling, though the touch be rough,
Our old souls are soft enough.

So we'll make a mellow hour:
Fill your pipe, and taste the wine
Warp your face, if it be sour,
I can spare a smile from mine;
If it sharpen up your wit,
Let me feel the edge of it
I have eager ears to lend,
Tom Van Arden, my old friend.

Tom Van Arden, my old friend,
Are we "lucky dogs," indeed?
Are we all that we pretend

In the jolly life we lead?
Bachelors, we must confess,
Boast of "single blessedness"
To the world, but not alone
Man's best sorrow is his own!

And the saddest truth is this,
Life to us has never proved
What we tasted in the kiss
Of the women we have loved:
Vainly we congratulate
Our escape from such a fate
As their lying lips could send,
Tom Van Arden, my old friend!

Tom Van Arden, my old friend,
Hearts, like fruit upon the stem,
Ripen sweetest, I contend,
As the frost falls over them:
Your regard for me to-day
Makes November taste of May,
And through every vein of rhyme
Pours the blood of summertime.

When our souls are cramped with youth
Happiness seems far away
In the future, while, in truth,
We look back on it to-day
Through our tears, nor dare to boast,
"Better to have loved and lost!"
Broken hearts are hard to mend,
Tom Van Arden, my old friend.

Tom Van Arden, my old friend,
I grow prosy, and you tire;
Fill the glasses while I bend
To prod up the failing fire . . .
You are restless: I presume
There's a dampness in the room.
Much of warmth our nature begs,
With rheumatics in our legs! . . .

Humph! the legs we used to fling
Limber-jointed in the dance,
When we heard the fiddle ring
Up the curtain of Romance,
And in crowded public halls
Played with hearts like jugglers'-balls.
Feats of mountebanks, depend!
Tom Van Arden, my old friend.

Tom Van Arden, my old friend,
Pardon, then, this theme of mine:
While the fire-light leaps to lend
Higher color to the wine,
I propose a health to those
Who have homes, and home's repose,
Wife- and child-love without end!
. . . Tom Van Arden, my old friend.

JUST TO BE GOOD

Just to be good
This is enough, enough!
O we who find sin's billows wild and rough,
Do we not feel how more than any gold
Would be the blameless life we led of old
While yet our lips knew but a mother's kiss?
Ah! though we miss
All else but this,
To be good is enough!

It is enough
Enough just to be good!
To lift our hearts where they are understood;
To let the thirst for worldly power and place
Go unappeased; to smile back in God's face
With the glad lips our mothers used to kiss.
Ah! though we miss
All else but this,
To be good is enough!

HOME AT NIGHT

When chirping crickets fainter cry,
And pale stars blossom in the sky,
And twilight's gloom has dimmed the bloom
And blurred the butterfly:

When locust-blossoms fleck the walk,
And up the tiger-lily stalk
The glow-worm crawls and clings and falls
And glimmers down the garden-walls:

When buzzing things, with double wings
Of crisp and raspish flutterings,
Go whizzing by so very nigh
One thinks of fangs and stings:

O then, within, is stilled the din

Of crib she rocks the baby in,
And heart and gate and latch's weight
Are lifted and the lips of Kate.

THE HOOSIER FOLK-CHILD
The Hoosier Folk-Child all unsung
Unlettered all of mind and tongue;
Unmastered, unmolested, made
Most wholly frank and unafraid:
Untaught of any school, unvexed
Of law or creed all unperplexed
Unsermoned, aye, and undefiled,
An all imperfect-perfect child
A type which (Heaven forgive us!) you
And I do tardy honor to,
And so, profane the sanctities
Of our most sacred memories.
Who, growing thus from boy to man,
That dares not be American?
Go, Pride, with prudent underbuzz
Go whistle! as the Folk-Child does.

The Hoosier Folk-Child's world is not
Much wider than the stable-lot
Between the house and highway fence
That bounds the home his father rents.
His playmates mostly are the ducks
And chickens, and the boy that "shucks
Corn by the shock," and talks of town,
And whether eggs are "up" or "down,"
And prophesies in boastful tone
Of "owning horses of his own,"
And "being his own man," and "when
He gets to be, what he'll do then."
Takes out his jack-knife dreamily
And makes the Folk-Child two or three
Crude corn-stalk figures, a wee span
Of horses and a little man.

The Hoosier Folk-Child's eyes are wise
And wide and round as Brownies' eyes:
The smile they wear is ever blent
With all-expectant wonderment,
On homeliest things they bend a look
As rapt as o'er a picture-book,
And seem to ask, whate'er befall,
The happy reason of it all:
Why grass is all so glad a green,
And leaves and what their lispings mean;

Why buds grow on the boughs, and why
They burst in blossom by and by
As though the orchard in the breeze
Had shook and popped its popcorn-trees,
To lure and whet, as well they might,
Some seven-league giant's appetite!

The Hoosier Folk-Child's chubby face
Has scant refinement, caste or grace,
From crown to chin, and cheek to cheek,
It bears the grimy water-streak
Of rinsings such as some long rain
Might drool across the window-pane
Wherethrough he peers, with troubled frown,
As some lorn team drives by for town.
His brow is elfed with wispish hair,
With tangles in it here and there,
As though the warlocks snarled it so
At midmirk when the moon sagged low,
And boughs did toss and skreek and shake,
And children moaned themselves awake,
With fingers clutched, and starting sight
Blind as the blackness of the night!

The Hoosier Folk-Child! Rich is he
In all the wealth of poverty!
He owns nor title nor estate,
Nor speech but half articulate,
He owns nor princely robe nor crown;
Yet, draped in patched and faded brown,
He owns the bird-songs of the hills
The laughter of the April rills;
And his are all the diamonds set.
In Morning's dewy coronet,
And his the Dusk's first minted stars
That twinkle through the pasture-bars,
And litter all the skies at night
With glittering scraps of silver light;
The rainbow's bar, from rim to rim,
In beaten gold, belongs to him.

JACK THE GIANT KILLER
Bad Boy's Version.

Tell you a story an' it's a fac':
Wunst wuz a little boy, name wuz Jack,
An' he had sword an' buckle an' strap
Maked of gold, an' a "'visibul cap;"
An' he killed Gi'nts 'at et whole cows

Th' horns an' all an' pigs an' sows!
But Jack, his golding sword wuz, oh!
So awful sharp 'at he could go
An' cut th' ole Gi'nts clean in two
Fore 'ey knowed what he wuz goin' to do!
An' one ole Gi'nt, he had four
Heads, and name wuz "Bumblebore"
An' he wuz feered o' Jack 'cause he,
Jack, he killed six, five, ten, three,
An' all o' th' uther ole Gi'nts but him:
An' thay wuz a place Jack haf to swim
'Fore he could git t' ole "Bumblebore"
Nen thay was "griffuns" at the door:
But Jack, he thist plunged in an' swum
Clean acrost; an' when he come
To th' uther side, he thist put on
His "'visibul cap," an' nen, dog-gone!
You could n't see him at all! An' so
He slewed the "griffuns" boff, you know!
Nen wuz a horn hunged over his head
High on th' wall, an' words 'at read,
"Whoever kin this trumput blow
Shall cause the Gi'nt's overth'ow!"
An' Jack, he thist reached up an' blowed
The stuffin' out of it! an' th'owed
Th' castul-gates wide open, an'
Nen tuck his gold sword in his han',
An' thist marched in t' ole "Bumblebore,"
An', 'fore he knowed, he put 'bout four
Heads on him an' chopped 'em off, too!
Wisht 'at I'd been Jack! don't you?

WHILE THE MUSICIAN PLAYED.

O it was but a dream I had
While the musician played!
And here the sky, and here the glad
Old ocean kissed the glade
And here the laughing ripples ran,
And here the roses grew
That threw a kiss to every man
That voyaged with the crew.

Our silken sails in lazy folds
Drooped in the breathless breeze:
As o'er a field of marigolds
Our eyes swam o'er the seas;
While here the eddies lisped and purled
Around the island's rim,
And up from out the underworld

We saw the mermen swim.

And it was dawn and middle-day
And midnight, for the moon
On silver rounds across the bay
Had climbed the skies of June
And there the glowing, glorious king
Of day ruled o'er his realm,
With stars of midnight glittering
About his diadem.

The seagull reeled on languid wing
In circles round the mast,
We heard the songs the sirens sing
As we went sailing past;
And up and down the golden sands
A thousand fairy throngs
Flung at us from their flashing hands
The echoes of their songs.

O it was but a dream I had
While the musician played
For here the sky, and here the glad
Old ocean kissed the glade;
And here the laughing ripples ran,
And here the roses grew
That threw a kiss to every man
That voyaged with the crew.

AUGUST

A day of torpor in the sullen heat
Of Summer's passion: In the sluggish stream
The panting cattle lave their lazy feet,
With drowsy eyes, and dream.

Long since the winds have died, and in the sky
There lives no cloud to hint of Nature's grief;
The sun glares ever like an evil eye,
And withers flower and leaf.

Upon the gleaming harvest-field remote
The thresher lies deserted, like some old
Dismantled galleon that hangs afloat
Upon a sea of gold.

The yearning cry of some bewildered bird
Above an empty nest, and truant boys
Along the river's shady margin heard
A harmony of noise

A melody of wrangling voices blent
With liquid laughter, and with rippling calls
Of piping lips and trilling echoes sent
To mimic waterfalls.

And through the hazy veil the atmosphere
Has draped about the gleaming face of Day,
The sifted glances of the sun appear
In splinterings of spray.

The dusty highway, like a cloud of dawn,
Trails o'er the hillside, and the passer-by,
A tired ghost in misty shroud, toils on
His journey to the sky.

And down across the valley's drooping sweep,
Withdrawn to farthest limit of the glade,
The forest stands in silence, drinking deep
Its purple wine of shade.

The gossamer floats up on phantom wing;
The sailor-vision voyages the skies
And carries into chaos everything
That freights the weary eyes:

Till, throbbing on and on, the pulse of heat
Increases, reaches, passes fever's height,
And Day sinks into slumber, cool and sweet,
Within the arms of Night.

TO HEAR HER SING

To hear her sing, to hear her sing
It is to hear the birds of Spring
In dewy groves on blooming sprays
Pour out their blithest roundelays.

It is to hear the robin trill
At morning, or the whip-poor-will
At dusk, when stars are blossoming
To hear her sing, to hear her sing!

To hear her sing it is to hear
The laugh of childhood ringing clear
In woody path or grassy lane
Our feet may never fare again.

Faint, far away as Memory dwells,
It is to hear the village bells

At twilight, as the truant hears
Them, hastening home, with smiles and tears.

Such joy it is to hear her sing,
We fall in love with everything
The simple things of every day
Grow lovelier than words can say.

The idle brooks that purl across
The gleaming pebbles and the moss,
We love no less than classic streams
The Rhines and Arnos of our dreams.

To hear her sing with folded eyes,
It is, beneath Venetian skies,
To hear the gondoliers' refrain,
Or troubadours of sunny Spain.

To hear the bulbul's voice that shook
The throat that trilled for Lalla Rookh:
What wonder we in homage bring
Our hearts to her to hear her sing!

BEING HIS MOTHER

Being his mother when he goes away
I would not hold him overlong, and so
Sometimes my yielding sight of him grows O
So quick of tears, I joy he did not stay
To catch the faintest rumor of them! Nay,
Leave always his eyes clear and glad, although
Mine own, dear Lord, do fill to overflow;
Let his remembered features, as I pray,
Smile ever on me! Ah! what stress of love
Thou givest me to guard with Thee thiswise:
Its fullest speech ever to be denied
Mine own, being his mother! All thereof
Thou knowest only, looking from the skies
As when not Christ alone was crucified.

JUNE AT WOODRUFF.

Out at Woodruff Place afar
From the city's glare and jar,
With the leafy trees, instead
Of the awnings, overhead;
With the shadows cool and sweet,
For the fever of the street;
With the silence, like a prayer,

Breathing round us everywhere.

Gracious anchorage, at last,
From the billows of the vast
Tide of life that comes and goes,
Whence and where nobody knows
Moving, like a skeptic's thought,
Out of nowhere into naught.
Touch and tame us with thy grace,
Placid calm of Woodruff Place!

Weave a wreath of beechen leaves
For the brow that throbs and grieves
O'er the ledger, bloody-lined,
'Neath the sun-struck window-blind!
Send the breath of woodland bloom
Through the sick man's prison room,
Till his old farm-home shall swim
Sweet in mind to hearten him!

Out at Woodruff Place the Muse
Dips her sandal in the dews,
Sacredly as night and dawn
Baptize lilied grove and lawn:
Woody path, or paven way
She doth haunt them night and day,
Sun or moonlight through the trees,
To her eyes, are melodies.

Swinging lanterns, twinkling clear
Through night-scenes, are songs to her
Tinted lilts and choiring hues,
Blent with children's glad halloos;
Then belated lays that fade
Into midnight's serenade
Vine-like words and zithern-strings
Twined through all her slumberings.

Blesséd be each hearthstone set
Neighboring the violet!
Blessed every rooftree prayed
Over by the beech's shade!
Blessed doorway, opening where
We may look on Nature there
Hand to hand and face to face
Storied realm, or Woodruff Place.

FARMER WHIPPLE - BACHELOR.
It's a mystery to see me a man o' fifty-four,

Who's lived a cross old bachelor fer thirty year' and more
A-lookin' glad and smilin'! And they's none o' you can say
That you can guess the reason why I feel so good to-day!

I must tell you all about it! But I'll have to deviate
A little in beginning so's to set the matter straight
As to how it comes to happen that I never took a wife —
Kind o' "crawfish" from the Present to the Springtime of my life!

I was brought up in the country: Of a family of five —
Three brothers and a sister, I'm the only one alive,
Fer they all died little babies; and 'twas one o' Mother's ways,
You know, to want a daughter; so she took a girl to raise.

The sweetest little thing she was, with rosy cheeks, and fat —
We was little chunks o' shavers then — about as high as that!
But someway we sort o' suited-like! and Mother she'd declare
She never laid her eyes on a more lovin' pair

Than we was! So we growed up side by side fer thirteen year',
And every hour of it she growed to me more dear!
W'y, even Father's dyin', as he did, I do believe
Warn't more affectin' to me than it was to see her grieve!

I was then a lad o' twenty; and I felt a flash o' pride
In thinkin' all depended on me now to pervide
Fer Mother and fer Mary; and I went about the place
With sleeves rolled up and workin', with a mighty smilin' face.

Fer sompin' else was workin'! but not a word I said
Of a certain sort o' notion that was runnin' through my head, —
"Someday I'd maybye marry, and a brother's love was one
Thing — a lover's was another!" was the way the notion run!

I remember onc't in harvest, when the "cradle-in'" was done —
When the harvest of my summers mounted up to twenty-one —
I was ridin' home with Mary at the closin' o' the day
A-chawin' straws and thinkin', in a lover's lazy way!

And Mary's cheeks was burnin' like the sunset down the lane:
I noticed she was thinkin', too, and ast her to explain —
Well — when she turned and kissed me, with her arm around me — law!
I'd a bigger load o' heaven than I had a load o' straw!

I don't p'tend to learnin', but I'll tell you what's a fac',
They's a mighty truthful sayin' somers in a almanack —
Er somers 'bout "puore happiness" — perhaps some folks'll laugh
At the idy — "only lastin' jest two seconds and a half."

But its jest as true as preachin'! fer that was a sister's kiss,
And a sister's lovin' confidence a-tellin' to me this:

"She was happy, bein' promised to the son o' farmer Brown."
And my feelin's struck a pardnership with sunset and went down!

I don't know how I acted, I don't know what I said,
Fer my heart seemed jest a-turnin' to an ice-cold lump o' lead;
And the hosses kind o' glimmered before me in the road,
And the lines fell from my fingers and that was all I knowed

Fer well, I don't know how long. They's a dim rememberence
Of a sound o' snortin' bosses, and a stake-and-ridered fence
A-whizzin' past, and wheat-sheaves a-dancin' in the air,
And Mary screamin' "Murder!" and a-runnin' up to where

I was layin' by the roadside, and the wagon upside down
A-leanin' on the gate-post, with the wheels a whirlin' round!
And I tried to raise and meet her, but I couldn't, with a vague
Sort o' notion comin' to me that I had a broken leg.

Well, the women nussed me through it; but many a time I'd sigh
As I'd keep a-gittin' better instid o' goin' to die,
And wonder what was left me worth livin' fer below,
When the girl I loved was married to another, don't you know!

And my thoughts was as rebellious as the folks was good and kind
When Brown and Mary married. Railly must a-been my mind
Was kindo' out o' kilter! fer I hated Brown, you see,
Worse'n pizen and the feller whittled crutches out fer me

And done a thousand little ac's o' kindness and respec'
And me a-wishin' all the time that I could break his neck!
My relief was like a mourner's when the funeral is done
When they moved to Illinois in the Fall o' Forty-one.

Then I went to work in airnest, I had nothin' much in view
But to drown out rickollections and it kep' me busy, too!
But I slowly thrived and prospered, tel Mother used to say
She expected yit to see me a wealthy man some day.

Then I'd think how little money was, compared to happiness
And who'd be left to use it when I died I couldn't guess!
But I've still kep' speculatin' and a-gainin' year by year,
Tel I'm payin' half the taxes in the county, mighty near!

Well! A year ago er better, a letter comes to hand
Astin' how I'd like to dicker fer some Illinois land
"The feller that had owned it," it went ahead to state,
"Had jest deceased, insolvent, leavin' chance to speculate,"

And then it closed by sayin' that I'd "better come and see."
I'd never been West, anyhow a most too wild fer me,
I'd allus had a notion; but a lawyer here in town

Said I'd find myself mistakend when I come to look around.

So I bids good-bye to Mother, and I jumps aboard the train,
A-thinkin' what I'd bring her when I come back home again
And ef she'd had an idy what the present was to be,
I think it's more 'n likely she'd a-went along with me!

Cars is awful tejus ridin', fer all they go so fast!
But finally they called out my stopping-place at last:
And that night, at the tavern, I dreamp' I was a train
O' cars, and skeered at sumpin', runnin' down a country lane!

Well, in the mornin' airly after huntin' up the man
The lawyer who was wantin' to swap the piece o' land
We started fer the country;' and I ast the history
Of the farm, its former owner, and so-forth, etcetery!

And, well, it was interestin', I su'prised him, I suppose,
By the loud and frequent manner in which I blowed my nose!
But his su'prise was greater, and it made him wonder more,
When I kissed and hugged the widder when she met us at the door!

It was Mary: They's a feelin' a-hidin' down in here
Of course I can't explain it, ner ever make it clear.
It was with us in that meeting I don't want you to fergit!
And it makes me kind o' nervous when I think about it yit!

I bought that farm, and deeded it, afore I left the town,
With "title clear to mansions in the skies," to Mary Brown!
And fu'thermore, I took her and the children, fer you see,
They'd never seed their Grandma and I fetched 'em home with me.

So now you've got an idy why a man o' fifty-four,
Who's lived a cross old bachelor fer thirty year' and more,
Is a-lookin' glad and smilin'! And I've jest come into town
To git a pair o' license fer to marry Mary Brown.

DAWN, NOON AND DEWFALL
I.
Dawn, noon and dewfall! Bluebird and robin
Up and at it airly, and the orchard-blossoms bobbin'!
Peekin' from the winder, half-awake, and wishin'
I could go to sleep agin as well as go a-fishin'!

II.
On the apern o' the dam, legs a-danglin' over,
Drowsy-like with sound o' worter and the smell o' clover:
Fish all out a visitin', 'cept some dratted minnor!
Yes, and mill shet down at last and hands is gone to dinner.

III.
Trompin' home acrost the fields: Lightnin'-bugs a-blinkin'
In the wheat like sparks o' things feller keeps a-thinkin':
Mother waitin' supper, and the childern there to cherr me!
And fiddle on the kitchen-wall a-jist a-eechin' fer me!

NESSMUK

I hail thee, Nessmuk, for the lofty tone
Yet simple grace that marks thy poetry!
True forester thou art, and still to be,
Even in happier fields than thou hast known.
Thus, in glad visions, glimpses am I shown
Of groves delectable, "preserves" for thee
Ranged but by friends of thine, I name thee three:

First, Chaucer, with his bald old pate new-grown
With changeless laurel; next, in Lincoln-green,
Gold-belted, bowed and bugled, Robin Hood;
And next, Ike Walton, patient and serene:
These three, O Nessmuk, gathered hunter-wise,
Are camped on hither slopes of Paradise
To hail thee first and greet thee, as they should.

AS MY UNCLE USED TO SAY

I've thought a power on men and things,
As my uncle ust to say,
And ef folks don't work as they pray, i jings!
W'y, they ain't no use to pray!
Ef you want somepin', and jes dead-set
A-pleadin' fer it with both eyes wet,
And tears won't bring it, w'y, you try sweat,
As my uncle ust to say.

They's some don't know their A, B, Cs,
As my uncle ust to say,
And yit don't waste no candle-grease,
Ner whistle their lives away!
But ef they can't write no book, ner rhyme
No ringin' song fer to last all time,
They can blaze the way fer the march sublime,
As my uncle ust to say.

Whoever's Foreman of all things here,
As my uncle ust to say,
He knows each job 'at we're best fit fer,
And our round-up, night and day:

And a-sizin' His work, east and west,
And north and south, and worst and best
I ain't got nothin' to suggest,
As my uncle ust to say.

THE SINGER

While with Ambition's hectic flame
He wastes the midnight oil,
And dreams, high-throned on heights of fame,
To rest him from his toil,

Death's Angel, like a vast eclipse,
Above him spreads her wings,
And fans the embers of his lips
To ashes as he sings.

A FULL HARVEST

Seems like a feller'd ort 'o jes' to-day
Git down and roll and waller, don't you know,
In that-air stubble, and flop up and crow,
Seein' sich craps! I'll undertake to say
There're no wheat's ever turned out thataway
Afore this season! Folks is keerless tho',
And too fergitful 'caze we'd ort 'o show
More thankfulness! Jes' looky hyonder, hey?
And watch that little reaper wadin' thue
That last old yaller hunk o' harvest-ground
Jes' natchur'ly a-slicin' it in-two
Like honey-comb, and gaumin' it around
The field like it had nothin' else to do
On'y jes' waste it all on me and you!

BLIND

You think it is a sorry thing
That I am blind. Your pitying
Is welcome to me; yet indeed,
I think I have but little need
Of it. Though you may marvel much
That we, who see by sense of touch
And taste and hearing, see things you
May never look upon; and true
Is it that even in the scent
Of blossoms we find something meant
No eyes have in their faces read,
Or wept to see interpreted.

And you might think it strange if now
I told you you were smiling. How
Do I know that? I hold your hand
Its language I can understand
Give both to me, and I will show
You many other things I know.
Listen: We never met before
Till now? Well, you are something lower
Than five-feet-eight in height; and you
Are slender; and your eyes are blue

Your mother's eyes, your mother's hair
Your mother's likeness everywhere
Save in your walk and that is quite
Your father's; nervous. Am I right?
I thought so. And you used to sing,
But have neglected everything
Of vocalism though you may
Still thrum on the guitar, and play
A little on the violin,
I know that by the callous in
The finger-tips of your left hand
And, by-the-bye, though nature planned
You as most men, you are, I see,
"Left-handed," too, the mystery
Is clear, though, your right arm has been
Broken, to "break" the left one in.
And so, you see, though blind of sight,
I still have ways of seeing quite
Too well for you to sympathize
Excessively, with your good eyes.
Though once, perhaps, to be sincere,
Within the whole asylum here,
From cupola to basement hall,
I was the blindest of them all!

Let us move further down the walk
The man here waiting hears my talk,
And is disturbed; besides, he may
Not be quite friendly anyway.
In fact (this will be far enough;
Sit down) the man just spoken of
Was once a friend of mine. He came
For treatment here from Burlingame
A rich though brilliant student there,
Who read his eyes out of repair,
And groped his way up here, where we
Became acquainted, and where he
Met one of our girl-teachers, and,
If you 'll believe me, asked her hand

In marriage, though the girl was blind
As I am and the girl declined.
Odd, wasn't it? Look, you can see
Him waiting there. Fine, isn't he?
And handsome, eloquently wide
And high of brow, and dignified
With every outward grace, his sight
Restored to him, clear and bright
As day-dawn; waiting, waiting still
For the blind girl that never will
Be wife of his. How do I know?
You will recall a while ago
I told you he and I were friends.
In all that friendship comprehends,
I was his friend, I swear! why now,
Remembering his love, and how
His confidence was all my own,
I hear, in fancy, the low tone
Of his deep voice, so full of pride
And passion, yet so pacified
With his affliction, that it seems
An utterance sent out of dreams
Of saddest melody, withal
So sorrowfully musical
It was, and is, must ever be
But I'm digressing, pardon me.
I knew not anything of love
In those days, but of that above
All worldly passion, for my art
Music, and that, with all my heart
And soul, blent in a love too great
For words of mine to estimate.
And though among my pupils she
Whose love my friend sought came to me
I only knew her fingers' touch
Because they loitered overmuch
In simple scales, and needs must be
Untangled almost constantly.
But she was bright in other ways,
And quick of thought, with ready plays
Of wit, and with a voice as sweet
To listen to as one might meet
In any oratorio
And once I gravely told her so,
And, at my words, her limpid tone
Of laughter faltered to a moan,
And fell from that into a sigh
That quavered all so wearily,
That I, without the tear that crept
Between the keys, had known she wept;
And yet the hand I reached for then

She caught away, and laughed again.
And when that evening I strolled
With my old friend, I, smiling, told
Him I believed the girl and he
Were matched and mated perfectly:
He was so noble; she, so fair
Of speech, and womanly of air;
He, strong, ambitious; she, as mild
And artless even as a child;
And with a nature, I was sure,
As worshipful as it was pure
And sweet, and brimmed with tender things
Beyond his rarest fancyings.
He stopped me solemnly. He knew,
He said, how good, and just, and true
Was all I said of her; but as
For his own virtues, let them pass,
Since they were nothing to the one
That he had set his heart upon;
For but that morning she had turned
Forever from him. Then I learned
That for a month he had delayed
His going from us, with no aid
Of hope to hold him, meeting still
Her ever firm denial, till
Not even in his new-found sight
He found one comfort or delight.
And as his voice broke there, I felt
The brother-heart within me melt
In warm compassion for his own
That throbbed so utterly alone.
And then a sudden fancy hit
Along my brain; and coupling it
With a belief that I, indeed,
Might help my friend in his great need,
I warmly said that I would go
Myself, if he decided so,
And see her for him that I knew
My pleadings would be listened to
Most seriously, and that she
Should love him, listening to me.
Go; bless me! And that was the last
The last time his warm hand shut fast
Within my own so empty since,
That the remembered finger-prints
I 've kissed a thousand times, and wet
Them with the tears of all regret!

I know not how to rightly tell
How fared my quest, and what befell
Me, coming in the presence of

That blind girl, and her blinder love.
I know but little else than that
Above the chair in which she sat
I leant reached for, and found her hand,
And held it for a moment, and
Took up the other, held them both
As might a friend, I will take oath:
Spoke leisurely, as might a man
Praying for no thing other than
He thinks Heaven's justice; She was blind,
I said, and yet a noble mind
Most truly loved her; one whose fond
Clear-sighted vision looked beyond
The bounds of her infirmity,
And saw the woman, perfectly
Modeled, and wrought out pure and true
And lovable. She quailed, and drew
Her hands away, but closer still
I caught them. "Rack me as you will!"
She cried out sharply "Call me 'blind'
Love ever is, I am resigned!
Blind is your friend; as blind as he
Am I but blindest of the three
Yea, blind as death, you will not see
My love for you is killing me!"

There is a memory that may
Not ever wholly fade away
From out my heart, so bright and fair
The light of it still glimmers there.
Why, it did seem as though my sight
Flamed back upon me, dazzling white
And godlike. Not one other word
Of hers I listened for or heard,
But I saw songs sung in her eyes
Till they did swoon up drowning-wise,
As my mad lips did strike her own
And we flashed one and one alone!
Ah! was it treachery for me
To kneel there, drinking eagerly
That torrent-flow of words that swept
Out laughingly the tears she wept?
Sweet words! O sweeter far, maybe,
Than light of day to those that see,
God knows, who did the rapture send
To me, and hold it from my friend.

And we were married half a year
Ago, and he is, waiting here,
Heedless of that or anything,
But just that he is lingering

To say good-bye to her, and bow
As you may see him doing now,
For there's her footstep in the hall;
God bless her! help him! save us all!

RIGHT HERE AT HOME

Right here at home, boys, in old Hoosierdom,
Where strangers allus joke us when they come,
And brag o' their old States and interprize
Yit settle here; and 'fore they realize,
They're "hoosier" as the rest of us, and live
Right here at home, boys, with their past fergive!

Right here at home, boys, is the place, I guess,
Fer me and you and plain old happiness:
We hear the World's lots grander, likely so,
We'll take the World's word fer it and not go.
We know its ways aint our ways, so we'll stay
Right here at home, boys, where we know the way.

Right here at home, boys, where a well-to-do
Man's plenty rich enough and knows it, too,
And's got a' extry dollar, any time,
To boost a feller up 'at wants to climb
And 's got the git-up in him to go in
And git there, like he purt'-nigh allus kin!

Right here at home, boys, is the place fer us!
Where folks' heart's bigger 'n their money-pu's';
And where a common feller's jes as good
As ary other in the neighborhood:
The World at large don't worry you and me
Right here at home, boys, where we ort to be!

Right here at home, boys, jes right where we air!
Birds don't sing any sweeter anywhere:
Grass don't grow any greener'n she grows
Acrost the pastur' where the old path goes,
All things in ear-shot's purty, er in sight,
Right here at home, boys, ef we size 'em right.

Right here at home, boys, where the old home-place
Is sacerd to us as our mother's face,
Jes as we rickollect her, last she smiled
And kissed us, dyin' so and rickonciled,
Seein' us all at home here, none astray
Right here at home, boys, where she sleeps to-day.

THE LITTLE FAT DOCTOR

He seemed so strange to me, every way
In manner, and form, and size,
From the boy I knew but yesterday,
I could hardly believe my eyes!

To hear his name called over there,
My memory thrilled with glee
And leaped to picture him young and fair
In youth, as he used to be.

But looking, only as glad eyes can,
For the boy I knew of yore,
I smiled on a portly little man
I had never seen before!

Grave as a judge in courtliness
Professor-like and bland
A little fat doctor and nothing less,
With his hat in his kimboed hand.

But how we talked old times, and "chaffed"
Each other with "Minnie" and "Jim"
And how the little fat doctor laughed,
And how I laughed with him!

"And it's pleasant," I thought, "though I yearn to see
The face of the youth that was,
To know no boy could smile on me
As the little fat doctor does!"

THE SHOEMAKER

Thou Poet, who, like any lark,
Dost whet thy beak and trill
From misty morn till murky dark,
Nor ever pipe thy fill:
Hast thou not, in thy cheery note,
One poor chirp to confer
One verseful twitter to devote
Unto the Shoe-ma-ker?

At early dawn he doth peg in
His noble work and brave;
And eke from cark and wordly sin
He seeketh soles to save;
And all day long, with quip and song,
Thus stitcheth he the way
Our feet may know the right from wrong,

Nor ever go a stray.

Soak kip in mind the Shoe-ma-ker,
Nor slight his lasting fame:
Alway he waxeth tenderer
In warmth of our acclaim;
Aye, more than any artisan
We glory in his art
Who ne'er, to help the under man,
Neglects the upper part.

But toe the mark for him, and heel
Respond to thee in kine
Or kid or calf, shouldst thou reveal
A taste so superfine:
Thus let him jest, join in his laugh
Draw on his stock, and be
A shoer'd there's no rival half
Sole liberal as he.

Then, Poet, hail the Shoe-ma-ker
For all his goodly deeds,
Yea, bless him free for booting thee
The first of all thy needs!
And when at last his eyes grow dim,
And nerveless drops his clamp,
In golden shoon pray think of him
Upon his latest tramp.

THE OLD RETIRED SEA CAPTAIN

The old sea captain has sailed the seas
So long, that the waves at mirth,
Or the waves gone wild, and the crests of these,
Were as near playmates from birth:
He has loved both the storm and the calm, because
They seemed as his brothers twain,
The flapping sail was his soul's applause,
And his rapture, the roaring main.

But now like a battered hulk seems he,
Cast high on a foreign strand,
Though he feels "in port," as it need must be,
And the stay of a daughter's hand
Yet ever the round of the listless hours,
His pipe, in the languid air
The grass, the trees, and the garden flowers,
And the strange earth everywhere!

And so betimes he is restless here

In this little inland town,
With never a wing in the atmosphere
But the wind-mill's, up and down;
His daughter's home in this peaceful vale,
And his grandchild 'twixt his knees
But never the hail of a passing sail,
Nor the surge of the angry seas!

He quits his pipe, and he snaps its neck
Would speak, though he coughs instead,
Then paces the porch like a quarter-deck
With a reeling mast o'erhead!
Ho! the old sea captain's cheeks glow warm,
And his eyes gleam grim and weird,
As he mutters about, like a thunder-storm,
In the cloud of his beetling beard.

ROBERT BURNS WILSON

What intuition named thee? Through what thrill
Of the awed soul came the command divine
Into the mother-heart, foretelling thine
Should palpitate with his whose raptures will
Sing on while daisies bloom and lavrocks trill
Their undulating ways up through the fine
Fair mists of heavenly reaches? Thy pure line
Falls as the dew of anthems, quiring still
The sweeter since the Scottish singer raised
His voice therein, and, quit of every stress
Of earthly ache and longing and despair,
Knew certainly each simple thing he praised
Was no less worthy, for its lowliness,
Than any joy of all the glory There.

TO THE SERENADER

Tinkle on, O sweet guitar,
Let the dancing fingers
Loiter where the low notes are
Blended with the singer's:
Let the midnight pour the moon's
Mellow wine of glory
Down upon him through the tune's
Old romantic story!

I am listening, my love,
Through the cautious lattice,
Wondering why the stars above
All are blinking at us;

Wondering if his eyes from there
Catch the moonbeam's shimmer
As it lights the robe I wear
With a ghostly glimmer.

Lilt thy song, and lute away
In the wildest fashion:
Pour thy rippling roundelay
O'er the heights of passion!
Flash it down the fretted strings
Till thy mad lips, missing
All but smothered whisperings,
Press this rose I'm kissing.

THE WIFE-BLESSÉD
I.
In youth he wrought, with eyes ablur,
Lorn-faced and long of hair
In youth, in youth he painted her
A sister of the air
Could clasp her not, but felt the stir
Of pinions everywhere.

II.
She lured his gaze, in braver days,
And tranced him sirenwise;
And he did paint her, through a haze
Of sullen paradise,
With scars of kisses on her face
And embers in her eyes.

III.
And now, nor dream nor wild conceit
Though faltering, as before
Through tears he paints her, as is meet,
Tracing the dear face o'er
With lilied patience meek and sweet
As Mother Mary wore.

SISTER JONES'S CONFESSION
I thought the deacon liked me, yit
I warn't adzackly shore of it
Fer, mind ye, time and time agin,
When jiners 'ud be comin' in,
I'd seed him shakin' hands as free
With all the sistern as with me!
But jurin' last Revival, where

He called on me to lead in prayer,
An' kneeled there with me, side by side,
A-whisper'n' "he felt sanctified
Jes' tetchin of my gyarment's hem,"
That settled things as fur as them-
Thare other wimmin was concerned!
And well! I know I must a-turned
A dozen colors! Flurried? la!
No mortal sinner never saw
A gladder widder than the one
A-kneelin' there and wonderun'
Who'd pray'. So glad, upon my word,
I railly could n't thank the Lord!

THE CURSE OF THE WANDERING FOOT
All hope of rest withdrawn me?
What dread command hath put
This awful curse upon me
The curse of the wandering foot!
Forward and backward and thither,
And hither and yon again
Wandering ever! And whither?
Answer them, God! Amen.

The blue skies are far o'er me
The bleak fields near below:
Where the mother that bore me?
Where her grave in the snow?
Glad in her trough of a coffin
The sad eyes frozen shut
That wept so often, often,
The curse of the wandering foot!

Here in your marts I care not
Whatsoever ye think.
Good folk many who dare not
Give me to eat and drink:
Give me to sup of your pity
Feast me on prayers! O ye,
Met I your Christ in the city
He would fare forth with me

Forward and onward and thither,
And hither again and yon,
With milk for our drink together
And honey to feed upon
Nor hope of rest withdrawn us,
Since the one Father put
The blesséd curse upon us

The curse of the wandering foot.

A MONUMENT FOR THE SOLDIERS
A monument for the Soldiers!
And what will ye build it of?
Can ye build it of marble, or brass, or bronze,
Outlasting the Soldiers' love?
Can ye glorify it with legends
As grand as their blood hath writ
From the inmost shrine of this land of thine
To the outermost verge of it?

And the answer came: We would build it
Out of our hopes made sure,
And out of our purest prayers and tears,
And out of our faith secure:
We would build it out of the great white truths
Their death hath sanctified,
And the sculptured forms of the men in arms,
And their faces ere they died.

And what heroic figures
Can the sculptor carve in stone?
Can the marble breast be made to bleed,
And the marble lips to moan?
Can the marble brow be fevered?
And the marble eyes be graved
To look their last, as the flag floats past,
On the country they have saved?

And the answer came: The figures
Shall all be fair and brave,
And, as befitting, as pure and white
As the stars above their grave!
The marble lips, and breast and brow
Whereon the laurel lies,
Bequeath us right to guard the flight
Of the old flag in the skies!

A monument for the Soldiers!
Built of a people's love,
And blazoned and decked and panoplied
With the hearts ye build it oft
And see that ye build it stately,
In pillar and niche and gate,
And high in pose as the souls of those
It would commemorate!

THE RIVAL

I so loved once, when Death came by I hid
 Away my face,
And all my sweetheart's tresses she undid
 To make my hiding-place.

The dread shade passed me thus unheeding; and
 I turned me then
To calm my love, kiss down her shielding hand
 And comfort her again.

And lo! she answered not: And she did sit
 All fixedly,
With her fair face and the sweet smile of it,
 In love with Death, not me.

IRY AND BILLY AND JO

Iry an' Billy an' Jo!
Iry an' Billy's the boys,
An' Jo's their dog, you know,
Their pictures took all in a row.
Bet they kin kick up a noise
Iry and Billy, the boys,
And that-air little dog Jo!

Iry's the one 'at stands
Up there a-lookin' so mild
An' meek with his hat in his hands,
Like such a 'bediant child
(Sakes-alive!) An' Billy he sets
In the cheer an' holds onto Jo an' sweats
Hisse'f, a-lookin' so good! Ho-ho!
Iry an' Billy an' Jo!

Yit the way them boys, you know,
Usen to jes turn in
An' fight over that dog Jo
Wuz a burnin'-shame-an'-a-sin !
Iry he'd argy 'at, by gee-whizz!
That-air little Jo-dog wuz his!
An' Billy he'd claim it wuzn't so
'Cause the dog wuz his'n! An' at it they'd go,
Nip-an'-tugg, tooth-an'-toenail, you know
Iry an' Billy an' Jo!

But their Pa (He wuz the marshal then)
He 'tended-like 'at he jerked 'em up;
An' got a jury o' Brickyard men

An' helt a trial about the pup:
An' he says he jes like to a-died
When the rest o' us town-boys testified
Regardin', you know,
Iry an' Billy an' Jo.

'Cause we all knowed, when the Gypsies they
Camped down here by the crick last Fall,
They brung Jo with 'em, an' give him away
To Iry an' Billy fer nothin' at all!
So the jury fetched in the verdict so
Jo he ain't neether o' theirn fer shore
He's both their dog, an' jes no more!
An' so
They've quit quarrelin' long ago,
Iry an' Billy an' Jo.

A WRAITH OF SUMMERTIME
In its color, shade and shine,
'T was a summer warm as wine,
With an effervescent flavoring of flowered bough and vine,
And a fragrance and a taste
Of ripe roses gone to waste,
And a dreamy sense of sun- and moon- and star-light interlaced.

'Twas a summer such as broods
O'er enchanted solitudes,
Where the hand of Fancy leads us through voluptuary moods,
And with lavish love out-pours
All the wealth of out-of-doors,
And woos our feet o'er velvet paths and honeysuckle floors.

'Twas a summertime long dead,
And its roses, white and red,
And its reeds and water-lilies down along the river-bed,
O they all are ghostly things
For the ripple never sings,
And the rocking lily never even rustles as it rings!

HER BEAUTIFUL EYES
O her beautiful eyes! they are as blue as the dew
On the violet's bloom when the morning is new,
And the light of their love is the gleam of the sun
O'er the meadows of Spring where the quick shadows run:
As the morn shirts the mists and the clouds from the skies
So I stand in the dawn of her beautiful eyes.

And her beautiful eyes are as midday to me,
When the lily-bell bends with the weight of the bee,
And the throat of the thrush is a-pulse in the heat,
And the senses are drugged with the subtle and sweet
And delirious breaths of the air's lullabies
So I swoon in the noon of her beautiful eyes.

O her beautiful eyes! they have smitten mine own
As a glory glanced down from the glare of The Throne;
And I reel, and I falter and fall, as afar
Fell the shepherds that looked on the mystical Star,
And yet dazed in the tidings that bade them arise
So I grope through the night of her beautiful eyes.

DOT LEEDLE BOY
Ot's a leedle Christmas story
Dot I told der leedle folks
Und I vant you stop dot laughin'
Und grackin' funny jokes'
So-help me Peter-Moses!
Ot's no time for monkeyshine',
Ober I vas told you somedings
Of dot leedle boy of mine!

Ot vas von cold Vinter vedder,
Ven der snow vas all about
Dot you have to chop der hatchet
Eef you got der saur kraut!
Und der cheekens on der hind-leg
Vas standin' in der shine
Der sun shmile out dot morning
On dot leedle boy of mine.

He vas yoost a leedle baby
Not bigger as a doll
Dot time I got acquaintet
Ach! you ought to heard 'im squall!
I grackys! dot's der moosic
Ot make me feel so fine
Ven first I vas been marriet
Oh, dot leedle boy of mine!

He look' yoost like his fader!
So, ven der vimmen said
"Vot a purty leedle baby!"
Katrina shake der head.
I dink she must a-notice
Dot der baby vas a-gryin',
Und she cover up der blankets

Of dot leedle boy of mine.

Vel, ven he vas got bigger,
Dot he grawl und bump his nose,
Und make der table over,
Und molasses on his glothes
Dot make 'im all der sveeter,
So I say to my Katrine
"Better you vas quit a-shpankin'
Dot leedle boy of mine!"

I vish you could a-seen id
Ven he glimb up on der chair
Und shmash der lookin' glasses
Ven he try to comb his hair
Mit a hammer! Und Katrina
Say "Dot's an ugly sign!"
But I laugh und vink my fingers
At dot leedle boy of mine.

But vonce, dot Vinter morning,
He shlip out in der snow
Mitout no stockin's on 'im.
He say he "vant to go
Und fly some mit der birdies!"
Und ve give 'im medi-cine
Ven he catch der "parrygoric"
Dot leedle boy of mine!

Und so I set und nurse 'im,
Vile der Christmas vas come roun',
Und I told 'im 'bout "Kriss Kringle,"
How he come der chimbly down:
Und I ask 'im eef he love 'im
Eef he bring 'im someding fine?
"Nicht besser as mein fader,"
Say dot leedle boy of mine.

Und he put his arms aroun' me
Und hug so close und tight,
I hear der gclock a-tickin'
All der balance of der night! . . .
Someding make me feel so funny
Ven I say to my Katrine
"Let us go und fill der stockin's
Of dot leedle boy of mine."

Veil. Ve buyed a leedle horses
Dot you pull 'im mit a shtring,
Und a leedle fancy jay-bird
Eef you vant to hear 'im sing

You took 'im by der top-knot
Und yoost blow in behine
Und dot make much spectakel
For dot leedle boy of mine!

Und gandles, nuts and raizens
Unt I buy a leedle drum
Dot I vant to hear 'im rattle
Ven der Gristmas morning come!
Und a leedle shmall tin rooster
Dot vould crow so loud und fine
Ven he sqveeze 'im in der morning,
Dot leedle boy of mine!

Und vile ve vas a-fixin'
Dot leedle boy vake out!
I fought he been a-dreamin'
"Kriss Kringle" vas about,
For he say "Dot's him! I see 'im
Mit der shtars dot make der shine!"
Und he yoost keep on a-gryin'
Dot leedle boy of mine,

Und gottin' vorse und vorser
Und tumble on der bed!
So ven der doctor seen id,
He kindo' shake his head,
Und feel his pulse und visper
"Der boy is a-dyin'."
You dink I could believe id?
Dot leedle boy of mine?

I told you, friends dot's someding,
Der last time dot he speak
Und say "Goot-bye, Kriss Kringle!"
Dot make me feel so veak
I yoost kneel down und drimble,
Und bur-sed out a-gryin'
"Mein Goit, mein Gott im Himmel!
Dot leedle boy, of mine!"

Der sun don't shine dot Gristmas!
. . . Eef dot leedle boy vould liff'd
No deefer-en'! for Heaven vas
His leedle Gristmas-gift! . . .
Und der rooster, und der gandy,
Und me und my Katrine
Und der jay-bird is a-vaiting
For dot leedle boy of mine.

DONN PIATT OF MAC-O-CHEE

I.

Donn Piatt of Mac-o-chee,
Not the one of History,
Who, with flaming tongue and pen,
Scathes the vanities of men;
Not the one whose biting wit
Cuts pretense and etches it
On the brazen brow that dares
Filch the laurel that it wears:
Not the Donn Piatt whose praise
Echoes in the noisy ways
Of the faction, onward led
By the statesman! But, instead,
Give the simple man to me,
Donn Piatt of Mac-o-chee!

II.

Donn Piatt of Mac-o-chee!
Branches of the old oak tree,
Drape him royally in fine
Purple shade and golden shine!
Emerald plush of sloping lawn
Be the throne he sits upon!
And, O Summer sunset, thou
Be his crown, and gild a brow
Softly smoothed and soothed and calmed
By the breezes, mellow-palmed
As Erata's white hand agleam
On the forehead of a dream.
So forever rule o'er me,
Donn Piatt of Mac-o-chee!

III.

Donn Piatt of Mac-o-chee:
Through a lilied memory
Plays the wayward little creek
Round thy home at hide-and-seek
As I see and hear it, still
Romping round the wooded hill,
Till its laugh-and-babble blends
With the silence while it sends
Glances back to kiss the sight,
In its babyish delight,
Ere it strays amid the gloom
Of the glens that burst in bloom
Of the rarest rhyme for thee,
Donn Piatt of Mac-o-chee!

IV.
Donn Piatt of Mac-o-chee!
What a darling destiny
Has been mine to meet him there
Lolling in an easy chair
On the terrace, while he told
Reminiscences of old
Letting my cigar die out,
Hearing poems talked about;
And entranced to hear him say
Gentle things of Thackeray,
Dickens, Hawthorne, and the rest,
Known to him as host and guest
Known to him as he to me
Donn Piatt of Mac-o-chee!

THEM FLOWERS

Take a feller 'at's sick and laid up on the shelf,
All shaky, and ga'nted, and pore
Jes all so knocked out he can't handle hisself
With a stiff upper-lip anymore;
Shet him up all alone in the gloom of a room
As dark as the tomb, and as grim,
And then take and send him some roses in bloom,
And you can have fun out o' him!

You've ketched him 'fore now when his liver was sound
And his appetite notched like a saw
A-mockin' you, mayby, fer romancin' round
With a big posy-bunch in yer paw;
But you ketch him, say, when his health is away,
And he's flat on his back in distress,
And then you kin trot out yer little bokay
And not be insulted, I guess!

You see, it's like this, what his weaknesses is,
Them flowers makes him think of the days
Of his innocent youth, and that mother o' his,
And the roses that she us't to raise:
So here, all alone with the roses you send
Bein' sick and all trimbly and faint,
My eyes is, my eyes is, my eyes is, old friend
Is a-leakin', I'm blamed ef they ain't!

THE QUIET LODGER

The man that rooms next door to me:

Two weeks ago, this very night,
He took possession quietly,
As any other lodger might
But why the room next mine should so
Attract him I was vexed to know,
Because his quietude, in fine,
Was far superior to mine.

"Now, I like quiet, truth to tell,
A tranquil life is sweet to me
But this," I sneered, "suits me too well.
He shuts his door so noiselessly,
And glides about so very mute,
In each mysterious pursuit,
His silence is oppressive, and
Too deep for me to understand."

Sometimes, forgetting book or pen,
I've found my head in breathless poise
Lifted, and dropped in shame again,
Hearing some alien ghost of noise
Some smothered sound that seemed to be
A trunk-lid dropped unguardedly,
Or the crisp writhings of some quire
Of manuscript thrust in the fire.

Then I have climbed, and closed in vain
My transom, opening in the hall;
Or close against the window-pane
Have pressed my fevered face, but all
The day or night without held not
A sight or sound or counter-thought
To set my mind one instant free
Of this man's silent mastery.

And often I have paced the floor
With muttering anger, far at night,
Hearing, and cursing, o'er and o'er,
The muffled noises, and the light
And tireless movements of this guest
Whose silence raged above my rest
Hoarser than howling storms at sea
The man that rooms next door to me.

But twice or thrice, upon the stair,
I've seen his face, most strangely wan,
Each time upon me unaware
He came, smooth'd past me, and was gone.
So like a whisper he went by,
I listened after, ear and eye,
Nor could my chafing fancy tell

The meaning of one syllable.

Last night I caught him, face to face,
He entering his room, and I
Glaring from mine: He paused a space
And met my scowl all shrinkingly,
But with full gentleness: The key
Turned in his door and I could see
It tremblingly withdrawn and put
Inside, and then the door was shut.

Then silence. Silence! why, last night
The silence was tumultuous,
And thundered on till broad daylight;
O never has it stunned me thus!
It rolls, and moans, and mumbles yet.
Ah, God! how loud may silence get
When man mocks at a brother man
Who answers but as silence can!

The silence grew, and grew, and grew,
Till at high noon to-day 'twas heard
Throughout the house; and men flocked through
The echoing halls, with faces blurred
With pallor, gloom, and fear, and awe,
And shuddering at what they saw
The quiet lodger, as he lay
Stark of the life he cast away.

So strange to-night those voices there,
Where all so quiet was before;
They say the face has not a care
Nor sorrow in it any more
His latest scrawl: "Forgive me - You
Who prayed, 'they know not what they do!'"
My tears wilt never let me see
This man that rooms next door to me!

THE WATCHES OF THE NIGHT
O the waiting in the watches of the night!
In the darkness, desolation, and contrition and affright;
The awful hush that holds us shut away from all delight:
The ever weary memory that ever weary goes
Recounting ever over every aching loss it knows
The ever weary eyelids gasping ever for repose
In the dreary, weary watches of the night!

Dark, stifling dark, the watches of the night!
With tingling nerves at tension, how the blackness flashes white

With spectral visitations smitten past the inner sight!
What shuddering sense of wrongs we've wrought
that may not be redressed
Of tears we did not brush away of lips we left unpressed,
And hands that we let fall, with all their loyalty unguessed!
Ah! the empty, empty watches of the night!

What solace in the watches of the night?
What frailest staff of hope to stay, what faintest shaft of light?
Do we dream and dare believe it, that by never weight of right
Of our own poor weak deservings, we shall win the dawn at last
Our famished souls find freedom from this penance for the past,
In a faith that leaps and lightens from the gloom
that flees aghast
Shall we survive the watches of the night?

One leads us through the watches of the night
By the ceaseless intercession of our loved ones lost to sight
He is with us through all trials, in His mercy and His might;
With our mothers there about Him, all our sorrow disappears,
Till the silence of our sobbing is the prayer the Master hears,
And His hand is laid upon us with the tenderness of tears
In the waning of the watches of the night.

HIS VIGIL

Close the book and dim the light,
I shall read no more to-night.
No, I am not sleepy, dear
Do not go: sit by me here
In the darkness and the deep
Silence of the watch I keep.
Something in your presence so
Soothes me as in long ago
I first felt your hand as now
In the darkness touch my brow;
I've no other wish than you
Thus should fold mine eyelids to,
Saying nought of sigh or tear
Just as God were sitting here.

THE PLAINT HUMAN

Season of snows, and season of flowers,
Seasons of loss and gain!
Since grief and joy must alike be ours,
Why do we still complain?

Ever our failing, from sun to sun,

O my intolerent brother:
We want just a little too little of one,
And much too much of the other.

BY ANY OTHER NAME
First the teacher called the roll,
Clos't to the beginnin',
"Addeliney Bowersox!"
Set the school a-grinnin'.
Wintertime, and stingin'-cold
When the session took up
Cold as we all looked at her,
Though she couldn't look up!

Total stranger to us, too
Country-folks ain't allus
Nigh so shameful unpolite
As some people call us!
But the honest facts is, then,
Addeliney Bower-
Sox's feelin's was so hurt
She cried half an hour!

My dest was acrost from her 'n:
Set and watched her tryin'
To p'tend she didn't keer,
And a kind o' dryin'
Up her tears with smiles - tel I
Thought, "Well, 'Addeliney
Bowersox' is plain, but she's
Purty as a piney!"

It's be'n many of a year
Sence that most oncommon
Cur'ous name o' Bowersox
Struck me so abomin-
Nubble and outlandish-like!
I changed it to Adde-
Liney Daubenspeck and that
Nearly killed her Daddy!

TO AN IMPORTUNATE GHOST
Get gone, thou most uncomfortable ghost!
Thou really dost annoy me with thy thin
Impalpable transparency of grin;
And the vague, shadowy shape of thee almost
Hath vext me beyond boundary and coast

Of my broad patience. Stay thy chattering chin,
And reel the tauntings of thy vain tongue in,
Nor tempt me further with thy vaporish boast
That I am helpless to combat thee! Well,
Have at thee, then! Yet if a doom most dire
Thou wouldst escape, flee whilst thou canst! Revile
Me not, Miasmic Mist! Rank Air! retire!
One instant longer an thou haunt'st me, I'll
Inhale thee, O thou wraith despicable!

THE QUARREL

They faced each other: Topaz-brown
And lambent burnt her eyes and shot
Sharp flame at his of amethyst.
"I hate you! Go, and be forgot
As death forgets!" their glitter hissed
(So seemed it) in their hatred. Ho!
Dared any mortal front her so?
Tempestuous eyebrows knitted down
Tense nostril, mouth, no muscle slack,
And black, the suffocating black
The stifling blackness of her frown!

Ah! but the lifted face of her!
And the twitched lip and tilted head!
Yet he did neither wince nor stir,
Only his hands clenched; and, instead
Of words, he answered with a stare
That stammered not in aught it said,
As might his voice if trusted there.

And what, what spake his steady gaze?
Was there a look that harshly fell
To scoff her? or a syllable
Of anger? or the bitter phrase
That myrrhs the honey of love's lips,
Or curdles blood as poison drips?
What made their breasts to heave and swell
As billows under bows of ships
In broken seas on stormy days?
We may not know, nor they indeed
What mercy found them in their need.

A sudden sunlight smote the gloom;
And round about them swept a breeze,
With faint breaths as of clover-bloom;
A bird was heard, through drone of bees,
Then, far and clear and eerily,
A child's voice from an orchard-tree

Then laughter, sweet as the perfume
Of lilacs, could the hearing see.
And he, O Love! he fed thy name
On bruiséd kisses, while her dim
Deep eyes, with all their inner flame,
Like drowning gems were turned on him.

THE OLD YEAR AND THE NEW
I.
As one in sorrow looks upon
The dead face of a loyal friend,
By the dim light of New Year's dawn
I saw the Old Year end.

Upon the pallid features lay
The dear old smile, so warm and bright
Ere thus its cheer had died away
In ashes of delight.

The hands that I had learned to love
With strength of passion half divine,
Were folded now, all heedless of
The emptiness of mine.

The eyes that once had shed their bright
Sweet looks like sunshine, now were dull,
And ever lidded from the light
That made them beautiful.

II.
The chimes of bells were in the air,
And sounds of mirth in hall and street,
With pealing laughter everywhere
And throb of dancing feet:

The mirth and the convivial din
Of revelers in wanton glee,
With tunes of harp and violin
In tangled harmony.

But with a sense of nameless dread,
I turned me, from the merry face
Of this newcomer, to my dead;
And, kneeling there a space,

I sobbed aloud, all tearfully:
By this dear face so fixed and cold,
O Lord, let not this New Year be
As happy as the old!

THE HEREAFTER

Hereafter! O we need not waste
Our smiles or tears, whatever befall:
No happiness but holds a taste
Of something sweeter, after all;
No depth of agony but feels
Some fragment of abiding trust,
Whatever death unlocks or seals,
The mute beyond is just.

JOHN BROWN

Writ in between the lines of his life-deed
We trace the sacred service of a heart
Answering the Divine command, in every part
Bearing on human weal: His love did feed
The loveless; and his gentle hands did lead
The blind, and lift the weak, and balm the smart
Of other wounds than rankled at the dart
In his own breast, that gloried thus to bleed.
He served the lowliest first, nay, them alone
The most despised that e'er wreaked vain breath
In cries of suppliance in the reign whereat
Red Guilt sate squat upon her spattered throne.
For these doomed there it was he went to death.
God! how the merest man loves one like that!

A CUP OF TEA

I have sipped, with drooping lashes,
Dreamy draughts of Verzenay;
I have flourished brandy-smashes
In the wildest sort of way;
I have joked with "Tom and Jerry"
Till wee hours ayont the twal'
But I've found my tea the very
Safest tipple of them all!

'Tis a mystical potation
That exceeds in warmth of glow
And divine exhilaration
All the drugs of long ago
All of old magicians' potions
Of Medea's filtered spells
Or of fabled isles and oceans
Where the Lotos-eater dwells!

Though I've reveled o'er late lunches
With blasé dramatic stars,
And absorbed their wit and punches
And the fumes of their cigars
Drank in the latest story,
With a cock-tail either end,
I have drained a deeper glory
In a cup of tea, my friend.

Green, Black, Moyune, Formosa,
Congou, Amboy, Pingsuey
No odds the name it knows, ah!
Fill a cup of it for me!
And, as I clink my china
Against your goblet's brim,
My tea in steam shall twine a
Fragrant laurel round its rim.

JUDITH

O her eyes are amber-fine
Dark and deep as wells of wine,
While her smile is like the noon
Splendor of a day of June.
If she sorrow, lo! her face
It is like a flowery space
In bright meadows, overlaid
With light clouds and lulled with shade
If she laugh, it is the trill
Of the wayward whippoorwill
Over upland pastures, heard
Echoed by the mocking-bird
In dim thickets dense with bloom
And blurred cloyings of perfume.
If she sigh, a zephyr swells
Over odorous asphodels
And wan lilies in lush plots
Of moon-drown'd forget-me-nots.
Then, the soft touch of her hand
Takes all breath to understand
What to liken it thereto!
Never roseleaf rinsed with dew
Might slip soother-suave than slips
Her slow palm, the while her lips
Swoon through mine, with kiss on kiss
Sweet as heated honey is.

THE ARTEMUS OF MICHIGAN

Grand Haven is in Michigan, and in possession, too,
Of as many rare attractions as our party ever knew:
The fine hotel, the landlord, and the lordly bill of fare,
And the dainty-neat completeness of the pretty waiters there;
The touch on the piano in the parlor, and the trill
Of the exquisite soprano, in our fancy singing still;
Our cozy room, its comfort, and our thousand grateful tho'ts,
And at our door the gentle face
Of
H.
Y.
Potts!

His artless observations, and his drollery of style,
Bewildered with that sorrowful serenity of smile
The eye's elusive twinkle, and the twitching of the lid,
Like he didn't go to say it and was sorry that he did.
O Artemus of Michigan! so worthy of the name,
Our manager indorses it, and Bill Nye does the same
You tickled our affection in so many tender spots
That even Recollection laughs
At
H.
Y.
Potts!

And hark ye! O Grand Haven! count your rare attractions o'er
The commerce of your ships at sea, and ships along the shore;
Your railroads, and your industries, and interests untold,
Your Opera House, our lecture, and the gate-receipts in gold!
Ay, Banner Town of Michigan! count all your treasures through
Your crowds of summer tourists, and your Sanitarium, too;
Your lake, your beach, your drives, your breezy groves
and grassy plots,
But head the list of all of these
With
H.
Y.
Potts!

THE HOODOO

Owned a pair o' skates onc't. Traded
Fer 'em, stropped 'em on and waded
Up and down the crick, a-waitin'
Tel she'd freeze up fit fer skatin'.
Mildest winter I remember
More like Spring- than Winter-weather!
Did n't frost tel bout December

Git up airly ketch a' feather
Of it, mayby, 'crost the winder
Sunshine swinge it like a cinder!

Well, I waited, and kep' waitin'!
Couldn't see my money's w'oth in
Them-air skates and was no skatin',
Ner no hint o' ice ner nothin'!
So, one day, along in airly
Spring, I swopped 'em off, and barely
Closed the dicker, 'fore the weather
Natchurly jes slipped the ratchet,
And crick, tail-race, all together,
Froze so tight cat couldn't scratch it!

THE RIVALS; OR THE SHOWMAN'S RUSE

A TRAGI-COMEDY, IN ONE ACT.

PERSONS REPRESENTED.

BILLY MILLER	)	The Rivals
JOHNNY WILLIAMS	)	

TOMMY WELLS   Conspirator

TIME Noon: SCENE Country Town. Rear-view of the Miller Mansion, showing Barn, with practical loft-window opening on alley-way, with colored-crayon poster beneath, announcing: "BILLY MILLER'S Big Show and Monstur Circus and Equareum! A shour-bath fer Each and All fer 20 pins. This Afternoon! Don't fer git the date!" Enter TOMMY WELLS and JOHNNY WILLIAMS, who gaze awhile at poster, TOMMY secretly smiling and winking at BILLY MILLER, concealed at loft-window above.

TOMMY (to JOHNNY).
Guess 'at Billy haint got back,
Can't see nothin' through the crack
Can't hear nothin' neither. No!
. . . Thinks he's got the dandy show,
Don't he?

JOHNNY (scornfully)
'Course' but what I care?
He haint got no show in there!
What's he got in there but that
Old hen, cooped up with a cat
An' a turkle, an' that thing
'At he calls his "circus-ring?"
"What a circus-ring!" I'd quit!
Bet mine's twic't as big as it!

TOMMY
Yes, but you got no machine
Wat you bathe with, painted green,
With a string to work it, guess!

JOHNNY (contemptuously)
Folks don't bathe in circuses!
Ladies comes to mine, you bet!
I' got seats where girls can set;
An' a dressin'-room, an' all,
Fixed up in my pony's stall
Yes, an' I' got carpet, too,
Fer the tumblers, and a blue
Center-pole!

TOMMY
Well, Billy, he's
Got a tight-rope an' trapeze,
An' a hoop 'at he jumps through
Head-first!

JOHNNY
Well, what's that to do
Lightin' on a pile o' hay?
Haint no actin' thataway!

TOMMY
Don't care what you say, he draws
Bigger crowds than you do, 'cause
Sense he started up, I know
All the fellers says his show
Is the best-un!

JOHNNY
Yes, an' he
Better not tell things on me!
His old circus haint no good!
'Cause he's got the neighborhood
Down on me he thinks 'at I'm
Goin' to stand it all the time;
Thinks ist 'cause my Pa don't 'low
Me to fight, he's got me now.
An' can say I lie, an' call
Me ist anything at all!
Billy Miller thinks I am
'Feared to say 'at he says "dam"
Yes, and worser ones! and I'm
Goin' to tell his folks sometime!
An' ef he don't shet his head
I'll tell worse 'an that he said

When he fighted Willie King
An' got licked like ever'thing!
Billy Miller better shin
Down his Daddy's lane agin,
Like a cowardy-calf, an' climb
In fer home another time!
Better

[Here BILLY leaps down from the loft upon his unsuspecting victim; and two minutes, later, JOHNNY, with the half of a straw hat, a bleeding nose, and a straight rent across one trouser-knee, makes his inglorious exit.]

WHAT CHRIS'MAS FETCHED THE WIGGINSES
Wintertime, er Summertime,
Of late years I notice I'm,
Kindo'-like, more subjec' to
What the weather is. Now, you
Folks 'at lives in town, I s'pose,
Thinks its bully when it snows;
But the chap 'at chops and hauls
Yer wood fer ye, and then stalls,
And snapps tuggs and swingletrees,
And then has to walk er freeze,
Haint so much "stuck on" the snow
As stuck in it. Bless ye, no!
When its packed, and sleighin's good,
And church in the neighborhood,
Them 'at's got their girls, I guess,
Takes 'em, likely, more er less,
Tell the plain facts o' the case,
No men-folks about our place
On'y me and Pap and he
'Lows 'at young folks' company
Allus made him sick! So I
Jes don't want, and jes don't try!
Chinkypin, the dad-burn town,
'S too fur off to loaf aroun'
Either day er night and no
Law compellin' me to go!
'Less 'n some Old-Settlers' Day,
Er big-doin's thataway
Then, to tell the p'inted fac',
I've went more so's to come back
By old Guthrie's 'still-house, where
Minors has got licker there
That's pervidin' we could show 'em
Old folks sent fer it from home!
Visit roun' the neighbors some,
When the boys wants me to come.

Coon-hunt with 'em; er set traps
Fer mussrats; er jes, perhaps,
Lay in roun' the stove, you know,
And parch corn, and let her snow!
Mostly, nights like these, you'll be
(Ef you' got a writ fer me)
Ap' to skeer me up, I guess,
In about the Wigginses.
Nothin' roun' our place to keep
Me at home with Pap asleep
'Fore it's dark; and Mother in
Mango pickles to her chin;
And the girls, all still as death,
Piecin' quilts. Sence I drawed breath
Twenty year' ago, and heerd
Some girls whispern' so's it 'peared
Like they had a row o' pins
In their mouth right there begins
My first rickollections, built
On that-air blame old piece-quilt!

Summertime, it's jes the same
'Cause I've noticed, and I claim,
As I said afore, I'm more
Subjec' to the weather, shore,
'Proachin' my majority,
Than I ever ust to be!
Callin' back last Summer, say,
Don't seem hardly past away
With night closin' in, and all
S' lonesome-like in the dew-fail:
Bats, ad-drat their ugly muggs!
Flickern' by; and lightnin'-bugs
Huckstern' roun' the airly night
Little sickly gasps o' light;
Whip-poor-wills, like all possessed,
Moanin' out their mournfullest;
Frogs and katydids and things
Jes clubs in and sings and sings
Their ding-dangdest! Stock's all fed,
And Pap's washed his feet fer bed;
Mother and the girls all down
At the milk-shed, foolin' roun'
No wunder 'at I git blue,
And lite out and so would you!
I caint stay aroun' no place
Whur they haint no livin' face:
'Crost the fields and thue the gaps
Of the hills they's friends, perhaps,
Waitin' somers, 'at kin be
Kindo' comfertin' to me!

Neighbors all 'is plenty good,
Scattered thue this neighberhood;
Yit, of all, I like to jes
Drap in on the Wigginses.
Old man, and old lady too,
'Pear-like, makes so much o' you,
Least, they've allus pampered me
Like one of the fambily.
The boys, too, 's all thataway
Want you jes to come and stay;
Price, and Chape, and Mandaville,
Poke, Chasteen, and "Catfish Bill"
Poke's the runt of all the rest,
But he's jes the beatinest
Little schemer, fer fourteen,
Anybody ever seen!
"Like his namesake," old man claims,
"Jeems K. Poke, the first o' names!
Full o' tricks and jokes and you
Never know what Poke's go' do!"
Genius, too, that-air boy is,
With them awk'ard hands o' his:
Gits this blame pokeberry-juice,
Er some stuff, fer ink and goose
Quill pen-p'ints: And then he'll draw
Dogdest pictures yevver saw!
Er make deers and eagles good
As a writin'-teacher could!
Then they's two twin boys they've riz
Of old Coonrod Wigginses
'At's deceast and glad of it,
'Cause his widder's livin' yit!

Course the boys is mostly jes'
Why I go to Wigginses.
Though Melviney, sometimes, she
Gits her slate and algebry
And jes' sets there ciphern' thue
Sums old Ray hisse'f caint do!
Jes' sets there, and tilts her chair
Forreds tel, 'pear-like, her hair
Jes' spills in her lap and then
She jes' dips it up again
With her hands, as white, I swan,
As the apern she's got on!

Talk o' hospitality!
Go to Wigginses with me
Overhet, or froze plum thue,
You'll find welcome waitin' you:

Th'ow out yer tobacker 'fore
You set foot acrost that floor,
"Got to eat whatever's set
Got to drink whatever's wet!"
Old man's sentimuns them's his
And means jes the best they is!
Then he lights his pipe; and she,
The old lady, presen'ly
She lights her'n; and Chape and Poke.
I haint got none, ner don't smoke,
(In the crick afore their door
Sorto so's 'at I'd be shore
Drownded mine one night and says
"I won't smoke at Wigginses!")
Price he's mostly talkin' 'bout
Politics, and "thieves turned out"
What he's go' to be, ef he
Ever "gits there" and "we'll see!"
Poke he 'lows they's blame few men
Go' to hold their breath tel then!
Then Melviney smiles, as she
Goes on with her algebry,
And the clouds clear, and the room's
Sweeter 'n crabapple-blooms!
(That Melviney, she' got some
Most surprisin' ways, I gum!
Don't 'pear like she ever says
Nothin', yit you'll listen jes
Like she was a-talkin', and
Half-way seem to understand,
But not quite, Poke does, I know,
'Cause he good as told me so,
Poke's her favo-rite; and he
That is, confidentially
He's my favo-rite and I
Got my whurfore and my why!)

I haint never ben no hand
Much at talkin', understand,
But they's thoughts o' mine 'at's jes
Jealous o' them Wigginses!
Gift o' talkin 's what they got,
Whether they want to er not
F'r instunce, start the old man on
Huntin'-scrapes, 'fore game was gone,
'Way back in the Forties, when
Bears stold pigs right out the pen,
Er went waltzin' 'crost the farm
With a bee-hive on their arm!
And sir, ping! the old man's gun
Has plumped-over many a one,

Firin' at him from afore
That-air very cabin-door!
Yes and painters, prowlin' 'bout,
Allus darkest nights. Lay out
Clost yer cattle. Great, big red
Eyes a-blazin' in their head,
Glittern' 'long the timber-line
Shine out some, and then un-shine,
And shine back. Then, stiddy! whizz!
'N there yer Mr. Painter is
With a hole bored spang between
Them-air eyes! Er start Chasteen,
Say, on blooded racin'-stock,
Ef you want to hear him talk;
Er tobacker how to raise,
Store, and k-yore it, so's she pays:
The old lady and she'll cote
Scriptur' tel she'll git yer vote!

Prove to you 'at wrong is right,
Jes as plain as black is white:
Prove when you're asleep in bed
You're a-standin' on yer head,
And yer train 'at's goin' West,
'S goin' East its level best;
And when bees dies, it's their wings
Wears out and a thousand things!
And the boys is "chips," you know;
"Off the old block." So I go
To the Wigginses, 'cause, jes
'Cause I like the Wigginses
Even ef Melviney she
Hardly 'pears to notice me!

Rid to Chinkypin this week
Yisterd'y. No snow to speak
Of, and didn't have no sleigh
Anyhow; so, as I say,
I rid in and froze one ear
And both heels and I don't keer!
"Mother and the girls kin jes
Bother 'bout their Chris'mases
Next time fer theirse'vs, I jack!"
Thinks-says-I, a-startin' back,
Whole durn meal-bag full of things
Wrapped in paper-sacks, and strings
Liable to snap their holt
Jes at any little jolt!
That in front o' me, and wind
With nicks in it, 'at jes skinned
Me alive! I'm here to say

Nine mile' hossback thataway
Would a-walked my log! But, as
Somepin' allus comes to pass,
As I topped old Guthrie's hill.
Saw a buggy, front the 'Still,
P'inted home'ards, and a thin
Little chap jes climbin' in.
Six more minutes I were there
On the groun's' And course it were
It were little Poke and he
Nearly fainted to see me!
"You ben in to Chinky, too?"
"Yes; and go' ride back with you,"
I-says-I. He he'pped me find
Room fer my things in behind
Stript my hoss's reins down, and
Put his mitt' on the right hand
So's to lead "Pile in!" says he,
"But you 've struck pore company!"
Noticed he was pale, looked sick,
Kindo-like, and had a quick
Way o' flickin' them-air eyes
O' his roun' 'at didn't size
Up right with his usual style
s' I, "You well?" He tried to smile,
But his chin shuck and tears come.
"I've run 'Viney 'way from home!"

Don't know jes what all occurred
Next ten seconds. Nary word,
But my heart jes drapt, stobbed thue,
And whirlt over and come to.
Wrenched a big quart bottle from
That fool-boy! and cut my thumb
On his little fiste-teeth, helt
Him snug in one arm, and felt
That-air little heart o' his
Churn the blood o' Wigginses
Into that old bead 'at spun
Roun' her, spilt at Lexington!
His k'niptions, like enough,
He'pped us both, though it was rough
Rough on him, and rougher on
Me when last his nerve was gone,
And he laid there still, his face
Fishin' fer some hidin'-place
Jes a leetle lower down
In my breast than he 'd yit foun'!

Last I kindo' soothed him, so's
He could talk. And what you s'pose

Them-air revelations of
Poke's was? . . . He'd ben writin' love-
Letters to Melviney, and
Givin her to understand
They was from "a young man who
Loved her," and "the violet's blue
'N sugar's sweet" and Lord knows what!
Tel, 'peared-like, Melviney got
S' interested in "the young
Man," Poke he says, 'at she brung
A' answer onc't fer him to take,
Statin' "she'd die fer his sake,"
And writ fifty xs "fer
Love-kisses fer him from her!"
I was standin' in the road
By the buggy, all I knowed
When Poke got that fer. "That's why,"
Poke says, "I 'fessed up the lie
Had to 'cause I see," says he,
"'Viney was in airnest she
Cried, too, when I told her. Then
She swore me, and smiled again,
And got Pap and Mother to
Let me hitch and drive her thue
Into Chinkypin, to be
At Aunt 'Rindy's Chris'mas-tree
That's to-night." Says I, "Poke durn
Your lyin' soul! 's that beau o' hern
That she loves. Does he live in
That hellhole o' Chinkypin?"
"No," says Poke, "er 'Viney would
Went some other neighborhood."
"Who is the blame whelp?" says I.
"Promised 'Viney, hope I'd die
Ef I ever told!" says Poke,
Pittiful and jes heart-broke
"'Sides that's why she left the place,
'She caint look him in the face
Now no more on earth!' she says. "
And the child broke down and jes
Sobbed! Says I, "Poke, I p'tend
T' be your friend, and your Pap's friend,
And your Mother's friend, and all
The boys' friend, little, large and small
The whole fambily's friend and you
Know that means Melviney, too.
Now, you hush yer troublin'! I'm
Go' to he'p friends ever' time
On'y in this case, you got
To he'p me and, like as not
I kin he'p Melviney then,

And we'll have her home again.
And now, Poke, with your consent,
I'm go' go to that-air gent
She's in love with, and confer
With him on his views o' her.
Blast him! give the man some show.
Who is he? I'm go' to know!"
Somepin' struck the little chap
Funny, 'peared-like. Give a slap
On his leg, laughed thue the dew
In his eyes, and says: "It's you!"

Yes, and 'cordin' to the last
Love-letters of ours 'at passed
Thue his hands we was to be
Married Chris'mas. "Gee-mun-nee!
Poke," says I, "it's suddent yit
We kin make it! You're to git
Up tomorry, say, 'bout three
Tell your folks you're go' with me:
We'll hitch up, and jes drive in
'N take the town o' Chinkypin!"

GO, WINTER!

Go, Winter! Go thy ways! We want again
The twitter of the bluebird and the wren;
Leaves ever greener growing, and the shine
Of Summer's sun not thine.

Thy sun, which mocks our need of warmth and love
And all the heartening fervencies thereof,
It scarce hath heat enow to warm our thin
Pathetic yearnings in.

So get thee from us! We are cold, God wot,
Even as thou art. We remember not
How blithe we hailed thy coming. That was O
Too long, too long ago!

Get from us utterly! Ho! Summer then
Shall spread her grasses where thy snows have been,
And thy last icy footprint melt and mold
In her first marigold.

ELIZABETH
May 1, 1891.
I.

Elizabeth! Elizabeth!
The first May-morning whispereth
Thy gentle name in every breeze
That lispeth through the young-leaved trees,
New raimented in white and green
Of bloom and leaf to crown thee queen;
And, as in odorous chorus, all
The orchard-blossoms sweetly call
Even as a singing voice that saith
Elizabeth! Elizabeth!

II.
Elizabeth! Lo, lily-fair,
In deep, cool shadows of thy hair,
Thy face maintaineth its repose.
Is it, O sister of the rose,
So better, sweeter, blooming thus
Than in this briery world with us?
Where frost o'ertaketh, and the breath
Of biting winter harrieth
With sleeted rains and blighting snows
All fairest blooms Elizabeth!

III.
Nay, then! So reign, Elizabeth,
Crowned, in thy May-day realm of death!
Put forth the scepter of thy love
In every star-tipped blossom of
The grassy dais of thy throne!
Sadder are we, thus left alone,
But gladder they that thrill to see
Thy mother's rapture, greeting thee.
Bereaved are we by life not death
Elizabeth! Elizabeth!

SLEEP

Orphaned, I cry to thee:
Sweet sleep! O kneel and be
A mother unto me!
Calm thou my childish fears:
Fold, fold mine eyelids to, all tenderly,
And dry my tears.

Come, Sleep, all drowsy-eyed
And faint with languor, slide
Thy dim face down beside
Mine own, and let me rest
And nestle in thy heart, and there abide,
A favored guest.

Good night to every care,
And shadow of despair!
Good night to all things where
Within is no delight!
Sleep opens her dark arms, and, swooning there,
I sob: Good night, good night!

DAN PAINE

Old friend of mine, whose chiming name
Has been the burthen of a rhyme
Within my heart since first I came
To know thee in thy mellow prime;
With warm emotions in my breast
That can but coldly be expressed,
And hopes and wishes wild and vain,
I reach my hand to thee, Dan Paine.

In fancy, as I sit alone
In gloomy fellowship with care,
I hear again thy cheery tone,
And wheel for thee an easy chair;
And from my hand the pencil falls
My book upon the carpet sprawls,
As eager soul and heart and brain,
Leap up to welcome thee, Dan Paine.

A something gentle in thy mein,
A something tender in thy voice,
Has made my trouble so serene,
I can but weep, from very choice.
And even then my tears, I guess,
Hold more of sweet than bitterness,
And more of gleaming shine than rain,
Because of thy bright smile, Dan Paine.

The wrinkles that the years have spun
And tangled round thy tawny face,
Are kinked with laughter, every one,
And fashioned in a mirthful grace.
And though the twinkle of thine eyes
Is keen as frost when Summer dies,
It can not long as frost remain
While thy warm soul shines out, Dan Paine.

And so I drain a health to thee;
May merry Joy and jolly Mirth
Like children clamber on thy knee,
And ride thee round the happy earth!

And when, at last, the hand of Fate
Shall lift the latch of Canaan's gate,
And usher me in thy domain,
Smile on me just as now, Dan Paine.

OLD WINTERS ON THE FARM
I have jest about decided
It 'ud keep a town-boy hoppin'
Fer to work all winter, choppin'
Fer a' old fire-place, like I did!
Lawz! them old times wuz contrairy!
Blame backbone o' winter, 'peared-like,
Wouldn't break! and I wuz skeerd-like
Clean on into Febuary!
Nothin' ever made we madder
Than fer Pap to stomp in, layin'
On a' extra fore-stick, sayin'
"Groun'hog's out and seed his shadder!"

AT UTTER LOAF.
I.
An afternoon as ripe with heat
As might the golden pippin be
With mellowness if at my feet
It dropped now from the apple-tree
My hammock swings in lazily.

II.
The boughs about me spread a shade
That shields me from the sun, but weaves
With breezy shuttles through the leaves
Blue rifts of skies, to gleam and fade
Upon the eyes that only see
Just of themselves, all drowsily.

III.
Above me drifts the fallen skein
Of some tired spider, looped and blown,
As fragile as a strand of rain,
Across the air, and upward thrown
By breaths of hayfields newly mown
So glimmering it is and fine,
I doubt these drowsy eyes of mine.

IV.
Far-off and faint as voices pent
In mines, and heard from underground,

Come murmurs as of discontent,
And clamorings of sullen sound
The city sends me, as, I guess,
To vex me, though they do but bless
Me in my drowsy fastnesses.

V.
I have no care. I only know
My hammock hides and holds me here
In lands of shade a prisoner:
While lazily the breezes blow
Light leaves of sunshine over me,
And back and forth and to and fro
I swing, enwrapped in some hushed glee,
Smiling at all things drowsily.

A LOUNGER

He leant against a lamp-post, lost
In some mysterious reverie:
His head was bowed; his arms were crossed;
He yawned, and glanced evasively:
Uncrossed his arms, and slowly put
Them back again, and scratched his side
Shifted his weight from foot to foot,
And gazed out no-ward, idle-eyed.

Grotesque of form and face and dress,
And picturesque in every way
A figure that from day to day
Drooped with a limper laziness;
A figure such as artists lean,
In pictures where distress is seen,
Against low hovels where we guess
No happiness has ever been.

A SONG OF LONG AGO

A song of Long Ago:
Sing it lightly, sing it low
Sing it softly, like the lisping of the lips we used to know
When our baby-laughter spilled
From the glad hearts ever filled
With music blithe as robin ever trilled!

Let the fragrant summer-breeze,
And the leaves of locust-trees,
And the apple-buds and blossoms, and the wings of honey-bees,
All palpitate with glee,

Till the happy harmony
Brings back each childish joy to you and me.

Let the eyes of fancy turn
Where the tumbled pippins burn
Like embers in the orchard's lap of tangled grass and fern,
There let the old path wind
In and out and on behind
The cider-press that chuckles as we grind.

Blend in the song the moan
Of the dove that grieves alone,
And the wild whir of the locust, and the bumble's drowsy drone;
And the low of cows that call
Through the pasture-bars when all
The landscape fades away at evenfall.

Then, far away and clear,
Through the dusky atmosphere,
Let the wailing of the kildee be the only sound we hear:
O sad and sweet and low
As the memory may know
Is the glad-pathetic song of Long Ago!

THE CHANT OF THE CROSS-BEARING CHILD
I bear dis cross dis many a mile.
O de cross-bearin' chile
De cross-bearin' chile!

I bear dis cross 'long many a road
Wha' de pink ain't bloom' an' de grass done mowed.
O de cross-bearin' chile
De cross-bearin' chile!

Hits on my conscience all dese days
Fo' ter bear de cross ut de good Lord lays
On my po' soul, an' ter lif my praise.
O de cross-bearin' chile
De cross-bearin' chile!

I 's nigh-'bout weak ez I mos' kin be,
Yit de Marstah call an' He say, "You 's free
Fo' ter 'cept dis cross, an' ter cringe yo' knee
To no n'er man in de worl' but me!"
O de cross-bearin' chile
De cross-bearin' chile!

Says you guess wrong, ef I let you guess
Says you 'spec' mo', an'-a you git less:

Says you go eas', says you go wes',
An' whense you fine de road ut you like bes'
You betteh take ch'ice er any er de res'!
O de cross-bearin' chile
De cross-bearin' chile!

He build my feet, an' He fix de signs
Dat de shoe hit pinch an' de shoe hit bines
Ef I on'y w'ah eights an-a wanter w'ah nines;
I hone fo' de rain, an' de sun hit shines,
An' whilse I hunt de sun, hits de rain I fines.
O-a trim my lamp, an-a gyrd my lines!
O de cross-bearin' chile
De cross-bearin' chile!

I wade de wet, an' I walk de dry:
I done tromp long, an' I done clim high;
An' I pilgrim on ter de jasper sky,
An' I taken de resk fo' ter cas' my eye
Wha' de Gate swing wide an' de Lord draw nigh,
An' de Trump hit blow, an' I hear de cry,
"You lay dat cross down by an' by!
O de Cross-bearin' Chile
Do Cross-bearin' Chile!"

THANKSGIVING

Let us be thankful, not only because
Since last our universal thanks were told
We have grown greater in the world's applause,
And fortune's newer smiles surpass the old

But thankful for all things that come as alms
From out the open hand of Providence:
The winter clouds and storms, the summer calms
The sleepless dread, the drowse of indolence.

Let us be thankful, thankful for the prayers
Whose gracious answers were long, long delayed,
That they might fall upon us unawares,
And bless us, as in greater need, we prayed.

Let us be thankful for the loyal hand
That love held out in welcome to our own,
When love and only love could understand
The need of touches we had never known.

Let us be thankful for the longing eyes
That gave their secret to us as they wept,
Yet in return found, with a sweet surprise,

Love's touch upon their lids, and, smiling, slept.

And let us, too, be thankful that the tears
Of sorrow have not all been drained away,
That through them still, for all the coming years,
We may look on the dead face of To-day.

AUTUMN

As a harvester, at dusk,
Faring down some woody trail
Leading homeward through the musk
Of may-apple and pawpaw,
Hazel-bush, and spice and haw,
So comes Autumn, swart and hale,
Drooped of frame and slow of stride.
But withal an air of pride
Looming up in stature far
Higher than his shoulders are;
Weary both in arm and limb,
Yet the wholesome heart of him
Sheer at rest and satisfied.

Greet him as with glee of drums
And glad cymbals, as he comes!
Robe him fair, O Rain and Shine.
He the Emperor, the King
Royal lord of everything
Sagging Plenty's granary floors
And out-bulging all her doors;
He the god of corn and wine,
Honey, milk, and fruit and oil
Lord of feast, as lord of toil
Jocund host of yours and mine!

Ho! the revel of his laugh!
Half is sound of winds, and half
Roar of ruddy blazes drawn
Up the throats of chimneys wide,
Circling which, from side to side,
Faces lit as by the Dawn,
With her highest tintings on
Tip of nose, and cheek, and chin
Smile at some old fairy-tale
Of enchanted lovers, in
Silken gown and coat of mail,
With a retinue of elves
Merry as their very selves,
Trooping ever, hand in hand,
Down the dales of Wonderland.

Then the glory of his song!
Lifting up his dreamy eyes
Singing haze across the skies;
Singing clouds that trail along
Towering tops of trees that seize
Tufts of them to stanch the breeze;
Singing slanted strands of rain
In between the sky and earth,
For the lyre to mate the mirth
And the might of his refrain:
Singing southward-flying birds
Down to us, and afterwards
Singing them to flight again;
Singing blushes to the cheeks
Of the leaves upon the trees
Singing on and changing these
Into pallor, slowly wrought,
Till the little, moaning creeks
Bear them to their last farewell,
As Elaine, the lovable,
Was borne down to Lancelot.
Singing drip of tears, and then
Drying them with smiles again.

Singing apple, peach and grape,
Into roundest, plumpest shape,
Rosy ripeness to the face
Of the pippin; and the grace
Of the dainty stamin-tip
To the huge bulk of the pear,
Pendant in the green caress
Of the leaves, and glowing through
With the tawny laziness
Of the gold that Ophir knew,
Haply, too, within its rind
Such a cleft as bees may find,
Bungling on it half aware.
And wherein to see them sip
Fancy lifts an oozy lip,
And the singer's falter there.

Sweet as swallows swimming through
Eddyings of dusk and dew,
Singing happy scenes of home
Back to sight of eager eyes
That have longed for them to come,
Till their coming is surprise
Uttered only by the rush
Of quick tears and prayerful hush;
Singing on, in clearer key,

Hearty palms of you and me
Into grasps that tingle still
Rapturous, and ever will!
Singing twank and twang of strings
Trill of flute and clarinet
In a melody that rings
Like the tunes we used to play,
And our dreams are playing yet!
Singing lovers, long astray,
Each to each, and, sweeter things
Singing in their marriage-day,
And a banquet holding all
These delights for festival.

THE TWINS

One 's the pictur' of his Pa,
And the other of her Ma
Jes the bossest pair o' babies 'at a mortal ever saw!
And we love 'em as the bees
Loves the blossoms of the trees,
A-ridin' and a-rompin' in the breeze!

One's got her Mammy's eyes
Soft and blue as Apurl-skies
With the same sort of a smile, like - Yes,
and mouth about her size,
Dimples, too, in cheek and chin,
'At my lips jes wallers in,
A-goin' to work, er gittin' home agin.

And the other. Well, they say
That he's got his Daddy's way
O' bein' ruther soberfied, er ruther extry gay,
That he either cries his best,
Er he laughs his howlin'est
Like all he lacked was buttons and a vest!

Look at her! and look at him!
Talk about yer "Cheru-bim!"
Roll 'em up in dreams together, rosy arm and chubby limb!
O we love 'em as the bees
Loves the blossoms of the trees,
A-ridin' and a-rompin' in the breeze!

BEDOUIN

O love is like an untamed steed!
So hot of heart and wild of speed,
And with fierce freedom so in love,

The desert is not vast enough,
With all its leagues of glimmering sands,
To pasture it! Ah, that my hands
Were more than human in their strength,
That my deft lariat at length
Might safely noose this splendid thing
That so defies all conquering!
Ho! but to see it whirl and reel
The sands spurt forward and to feel
The quivering tension of the thong
That throned me high, with shriek and song!
To grapple tufts of tossing mane
To spurn it to its feet again,
And then, sans saddle, rein or bit,
To lash the mad life out of it!

TUGG MARTIN.

I.
Tugg Martin's tough. No doubt o' that!
And down there at
The town he come from word's bin sent
Advisin' this-here Settle-ment
To kindo' humor Tugg, and not
To git him hot
Jest pass his imperfections by,
And he's as good as pie!

II.
They claim he's wanted back there. Yit
The officers they mostly quit
Insistin' when
They notice Tugg's so back'ard, and
Sorto' gives 'em to understand
He druther not! A Deputy
(The slickest one you ever see!)
Tackled him last "disguisin' then,"
As Tugg says, "as a gentlemen!"
You 'd ort o' hear Tugg tell it! My!
I thought I'd die!

III.
The way it wuz; Tugg and the rest
The boys wuz jest
A-kindo' gittin' thawed out, down
At "Guss's Place," fur-end o' town,
One night, when, first we knowed,
Some feller rode
Up in a buggy at the door,
And hollered fer some one to come

And fetch him some
Red-licker out. And whirped and swore
That colt he drove wuz "Thompson's" shore!

IV.
Guss went out, and come in agin
And filled a pint and tuck it out
Stayed quite a spell, then peeked back in,
Half-hid-like where the light wuz dim,
And jieuked his head
At Tugg and said,
"Come out a minute here's a gent
Wants you to take a drink with him."

V.
Well Tugg laid down his cards and went
In fact, we all
Got up, you know,
Startin' to go
When in reels Guss aginst the wall,
As white as snow,
Gaspin', "He's tuck Tugg! wher's my gun?"
And-sir, outside we heerd
The hoss snort and kick up his heels
Like he wuz skeerd,
And then the buggy-wheels
Scrape and then Tugg's voice hollerun',
"I'm bested! Good-bye, fellers!" . . . 'Peared
S' all-fired suddent,
Nobody couldn't
Jest git it fixed, tel hoss and man,
Buggy and Tugg, off through the dark
Went like the devil beatin' tan-
Bark!

VI.
What could we do? . . . We filed back to
The bar: And Guss jest looked at us,
And we looked back "The same as you,"
Still sayin' nothin' And the sap
It stood in every eye,
And every hat and cap
Went off, as we teched glasses solemnly,
And Guss says-he:
"Ef it's 'good-bye' with Tugg, fer shore, I say
God bless him! Er ef they
Aint railly no need to pray,
I'm not reniggin! board's the play,
And here's God bless him, anyway!"

VII.

It must a-bin an hour er so
We all set there,
Talkin o' pore
Old Tugg, you know,
'At never, wuz ketched up before
When all slow-like, the door
Knob turned and Tugg come shamblin' in,
Hand-cuffed' 'at's what he wuz, I swear!
Yit smilin,' like he hadn't bin
Away at all! And when we ast him where
The Deputy wuz at, "I don't know where," Tugg said,
"All I know is he's dead."

LET US FORGET
Let us forget. What matters it that we
Once reigned o'er happy realms of long-ago,
And talked of love, and let our voices low,
And ruled for some brief sessions royally?
What if we sung, or laughed, or wept maybe?
It has availed not anything, and so
Let it go by that we may better know
How poor a thing is lost to you and me.
But yesterday I kissed your lips, and yet
Did thrill you not enough to shake the dew
From your drenched lids and missed, with no regret,
Your kiss shot back, with sharp breaths failing you;
And so, to-day, while our worn eyes are wet
With all this waste of tears, let us forget!

JOHN ALDEN AND PERCILLY
We got up a Christmas-doin's
Last Christmas Eve
Kindo' dimonstration
'At I railly believe
Give more satisfaction
Take it up and down
Than ary intertainment
Ever come to town!

Railly was a theater
That's what it was,
But, bein' in the church, you know,
We had a "Santy Clause"
So 's to git the old folks
To patternize, you see,
And back the institootion up
Kindo' morally.

Schoolteacher writ the thing
(Was a friend o' mine),
Got it out o' Longfeller's
Pome "Evangeline"
Er some'rs 'bout the Purituns .
Anyway, the part
"John Alden" fell to me
And learnt it all by heart!

Claircy was "Percilly"
(Schoolteacher 'lowed
Me and her could act them two
Best of all the crowd)
Then blame ef he didn't
Git her Pap, i jing!
To take the part o' "Santy Clause,"
To wind up the thing.

Law! the fun o' practisun!
Was a week er two
Me and Claircy didn't have
Nothin' else to do!
Kep' us jes a-meetin' round,
Kindo' here and there,
Ever' night rehearsin'-like,
And gaddin' ever'where!

Game was wo'th the candle, though!
Christmas Eve at last
Rolled around. And 'tendance jes
Couldn't been surpassed!
Neighbors from the country
Come from Clay and Rush
Yes, and 'crost the county-line
Clean from Puckerbrush!

Meetin'-house jes trimbled
As "Old Santy" went
Round amongst the childern,
With their pepperment
And sassafrac and wintergreen
Candy, and "a ball
O' popcorn," the preacher 'nounced,
"Free fer each and all!"

Schoolteacher suddently
Whispered in my ear,
"Guess I got you: Christmas-gift!
Christmas is here!"
I give him a gold pen,

And case to hold the thing,
And Claircy whispered "Christmas-gift!"
And I give her a ring.

"And now," says I, "jes watch me
Christmas-gift," says I,
"I'm a-goin' to git one
'Santy's' comin' by!"
Then I rech and grabbed him:
And, as you'll infer,
'Course I got the old man's,
And he gimme her!

REACH YOUR HAND TO ME
Reach your hand to me, my friend,
With its heartiest caress
Sometime there will come an end
To its present faithfulness
Sometime I may ask in vain
For the touch of it again,
When between us land or sea
Holds it ever back from me.

Sometime I may need it so,
Groping somewhere in the night,
It will seem to me as though
Just a touch, however light,
Would make all the darkness day,
And along some sunny way
Lead me through an April-shower
Of my tears to this fair hour.

O the present is too sweet
To go on forever thus!
Round the corner of the street
Who can say what waits for us?
Meeting, greeting, night and day,
Faring each the self-same way
Still somewhere the path must end.
Reach your hand to me, my friend!

THE ROSE
It tossed its head at the wooing breeze;
And the sun, like a bashful swain,
Beamed on it through the waving frees
With a passion all in vain,
For my rose laughed in a crimson glee,

And hid in the leaves in wait for me.

The honey-bee came there to sing
His love through the languid hours,
And vaunt of his hives, as a proud old king
Might boast of his palace-towers:
But my rose bowed in a mockery,
And hid in the leaves in wait for me.

The humming-bird, like a courtier gay,
Dipped down with a dalliant song,
And twanged his wings through the roundelay
Of love the whole day long:
Yet my rose turned from his minstrelsy
And hid in the leaves in wait for me.

The firefly came in the twilight dim
My red, red rose to woo
Till quenched was the flame of love in him,
And the light of his lantern too,
As my rose wept with dew-drops three
And hid in the leaves in wait for me.

And I said: I will cult my own sweet rose
Some day I will claim as mine
The priceless worth of the flower that knows
No change, but a bloom divine
The bloom of a fadeless constancy
That hides in the leaves in wait for me!

But time passed by in a strange disguise,
And I marked it not, but lay
In a lazy dream, with drowsy eyes,
Till the summer slipped away,
And a chill wind sang in a minor key:
"Where is the rose that waits for thee?"

I dream to-day, o'er a purple stain
Of bloom on a withered stalk,
Pelted down by the autumn rain
In the dust of the garden-walk,
That an Angel-rose in the world to be
Will hide in the leaves in wait for me.

MY FRIEND
"He is my friend," I said,
"Be patient!" Overhead
The skies were drear and dim;
And lo! the thought of him

Smited on my heart and then
The sun shone out again!

"He is my friend!" The words
Brought summer and the birds;
And all my winter-time
Thawed into running rhyme
And rippled into song,
Warm, tender, brave, and strong.

And so it sings to-day.
So may it sing alway!
Though waving grasses grow
Between, and lilies blow
Their trills of perfume clear
As laughter to the ear,
Let each mute measure end
With "Still he is thy friend."

SUSPENSE

A woman's figure, on a ground of night
Inlaid with sallow stars that dimly stare
Down in the lonesome eyes, uplifted there
As in vague hope some alien lance of light
Might pierce their woe. The tears that blind her sight
The salt and bitter blood of her despair
Her hands toss back through torrents of her hair
And grip toward God with anguish infinite.
And O the carven mouth, with all its great
Intensity of longing frozen fast
In such a smile as well may designate
The slowly-murdered heart, that, to the last,
Conceals each newer wound, and back at Fate
Throbs Love's eternal lie "Lo, I can wait!"

THE PASSING OF A HEART

O touch me with your hands
For pity's sake!
My brow throbs ever on with such an ache
As only your cool touch may take away;
And so, I pray
You, touch me with your hands!

Touch, touch me with your hands.
Smooth back the hair
You once caressed, and kissed, and called so fair
That I did dream its gold would wear alway,

And lo, to-day
O touch me with your hands!

Just touch me with your hands,
And let them press
My weary eyelids with the old caress,
And lull me till I sleep. Then go your way,
That Death may say:
He touched her with his hands.

BY HER WHITE BED

By her white bed I muse a little space:
She fell asleep not very long ago,
And yet the grass was here and not the snow
The leaf, the bud, the blossom, and her face!
Midsummer's heaven above us, and the grace
Of Lovers own day, from dawn to afterglow;
The fireflies' glimmering, and the sweet and low
Plaint of the whip-poor-wills, and every place
In thicker twilight for the roses' scent.
Then night. She slept in such tranquility,
I walk atiptoe still, nor dare to weep,
Feeling, in all this hush, she rests content
That though God stood to wake her for me, she
Would mutely plead: "Nay, Lord! Let him so sleep."

WE TO SIGH INSTEAD OF SING

"Rain and rain! and rain and rain!"
Yesterday we muttered
Grimly as the grim refrain
That the thunders uttered:
All the heavens under cloud
All the sunshine sleeping;
All the grasses limply bowed
With their weight of weeping.

Sigh and sigh! and sigh and sigh!
Never end of sighing;
Rain and rain for our reply
Hopes half-drowned and dying;
Peering through the window-pane,
Naught but endless raining
Endless sighing, and, as vain,
Endlessly complaining.

Shine and shine! and shine and shine!
Ah! to-day the splendor!

All this glory yours and mine
God! but God is tender!
We to sigh instead of sing,
Yesterday, in sorrow,
While the Lord was fashioning
This for our To-morrow!

THE BLOSSOMS ON THE TREES
Blossoms crimson, white, or blue,
Purple, pink, and every hue,
From sunny skies, to tintings drowned
In dusky drops of dew,
I praise you all, wherever found,
And love you through and through;
But, Blossoms On The Trees,
With your breath upon the breeze,
There's nothing all the world around
As half as sweet as you!

Could the rhymer only wring
All the sweetness to the lees
Of all the kisses clustering
In juicy Used-to-bes,
To dip his rhymes therein and sing
The blossoms on the trees,
"O Blossoms on the Trees,"
He would twitter, trill and coo,
"However sweet, such songs as these
Are not as sweet as you:
For you are blooming melodies
The eyes may listen to!"

A DISCOURAGING MODEL
Just the airiest, fairiest slip of a thing,
With a Gainsborough hat, like a butterfly's wing,
Tilted up at one side with the jauntiest air,
And a knot of red roses sown in under there
Where the shadows are lost in her hair.

Then a cameo face, carven in on a ground
Of that shadowy hair where the roses are wound;
And the gleam of a smile O as fair and as faint
And as sweet as the masters of old used to paint
Round the lips of their favorite saint!

And that lace at her throat and the fluttering hands
Snowing there, with a grace that no art understands,

The flakes of their touches first fluttering at
The bow, then the roses, the hair and then that
Little tilt of the Gainsborough hat.

O what artist on earth with a model like this,
Holding not on his palette the tint of a kiss,
Nor a pigment to hint of the hue of her hair,
Nor the gold of her smile, O what artist could dare
To expect a result half so fair?

LAST NIGHT - AND THIS
Last night, how deep the darkness was!
And well I knew its depths, because
I waded it from shore to shore,
Thinking to reach the light no more.

She would not even touch my hand.
The winds rose and the cedars fanned
The moon out, and the stars fled back
In heaven and hid and all was black!

But ah! To-night a summons came,
Signed with a teardrop for a name,
For as I wondering kissed it, lo,
A line beneath it told me so.

And now the moon hangs over me
A disk of dazzling brilliancy,
And every star-tip stabs my sight
With splintered glitterings of light!

SEPTEMBER DARK
I.
The air falls chill;
The whip-poor-will
Pipes lonesomely behind the hill:
The dusk grows dense,
The silence tense;
And lo, the katydids commence.

II.
Through shadowy rifts
Of woodland, lifts
The low, slow moon, and upward drifts,
While left and right
The fireflies' light
Swirls eddying in the skirts of Night.

III.
O Cloudland, gray
And level, lay
Thy mists across the face of Day!
At foot and head,
Above the dead,
O Dews, weep on uncomforted!

A GLIMPSE OF PAN

I caught but a glimpse of him. Summer was here,
And I strayed from the town and its dust and heat
And walked in a wood, while the noon was near,
Where the shadows were cool, and the atmosphere
Was misty with fragrances stirred by my feet
From surges of blossoms that billowed sheer
O'er the grasses, green and sweet.

And I peered through a vista of leaning trees,
Tressed with long tangles of vines that swept
To the face of a river, that answered these
With vines in the wave like the vines in the breeze,
Till the yearning lips of the ripples crept
And kissed them, with quavering ecstacies,
And gurgled and laughed and wept.

And there, like a dream in a swoon, I swear
I saw Pan lying, his limbs in the dew
And the shade, and his face in the dazzle and glare
Of the glad sunshine; while everywhere,
Over, across, and around him blew
Filmy dragonflies hither and there,
And little white butterflies, two and two,
In eddies of odorous air.

OUT OF NAZARETH

"He shall sleep unscathed of thieves
Who loves Allah and believes."
Thus heard one who shared the tent,
In the far-off Orient,
Of the Bedouin ben Ahrzz
Nobler never loved the stars
Through the palm-leaves nigh the dim
Dawn his courser neighed to him!

He said: "Let the sands be swarmed
With such thieves as I, and thou

Shalt at morning rise, unharmed,
Light as eyelash to the brow
Of thy camel, amber-eyed,
Ever munching either side,
Striding still, with nestled knees,
Through the midnight's oases.

"Who can rob thee an thou hast
More than this that thou hast cast
At my feet this dust of gold?
Simply this and that, all told!
Hast thou not a treasure of
Such a thing as men call love?

"Can the dusky band I lead
Rob thee of thy daily need
Of a whiter soul, or steal
What thy lordly prayers reveal?
Who could be enriched of thee
By such hoard of poverty
As thy niggard hand pretends
To dole me thy worst of friends?
Therefore shouldst thou pause to bless
One indeed who blesses thee;
Robbing thee, I dispossess
But myself. Pray thou for me!"

He shall sleep unscathed of thieves
Who loves Allah and believes.

THE WANDERING JEW

The stars are failing, and the sky
Is like a field of faded flowers;
The winds on weary wings go by;
The moon hides, and the tempest lowers;
And still through every clime and age
I wander on a pilgrimage
That all men know an idle quest,
For that the goal I seek is REST!

I hear the voice of summer streams,
And, following, I find the brink
Of cooling springs, with childish dreams
Returning as I bend to drink
But suddenly, with startled eyes,
My face looks on its grim disguise
Of long gray beard; and so, distressed,
I hasten on, nor taste of rest.

I come upon a merry group
Of children in the dusky wood,
Who answer back the owlet's whoop,
That laughs as it had understood;
And I would pause a little space,
But that each happy blossom-face
Is like to one His hands have blessed
Who sent me forth in search of rest.

Sometimes I fain would stay my feet
In shady lanes, where huddled kine
Couch in the grasses cool and sweet,
And lift their patient eyes to mine;
But I, for thoughts that ever then
Go back to Bethlehem again,
Must needs fare on my weary quest,
And weep for very need of rest.

Is there no end? I plead in vain:
Lost worlds nor living answer me.
Since Pontius Pilate's awful reign
Have I not passed eternity?
Have I not drank the fetid breath
Of every fevered phase of death,
And come unscathed through every pest
And scourge and plague that promised rest?

Have I not seen the stars go out
That shed their light o'er Galilee,
And mighty kingdoms tossed about
And crumbled clod-like in the sea?
Dead ashes of dead ages blow
And cover me like drifting snow,
And time laughs on as 'twere a jest
That I have any need of rest.

LONGFELLOW
The winds have talked with him confidingly;
The trees have whispered to him; and the night
Hath held him gently as a mother might,
And taught him all sad tones of melody:
The mountains have bowed to him; and the sea,
In clamorous waves, and murmurs exquisite,
Hath told him all her sorrow and delight
Her legends fair, her darkest mystery.
His verse blooms like a flower, night and day;
Bees cluster round his rhymes; and twitterings
Of lark and swallow, in an endless May,
Are mingling with the tender songs he sings.

Nor shall he cease to sing in every lay
Of Nature's voice he sings and will alway.

JOHN MCKEEN

John McKeen, in his rusty dress,
His loosened collar, and swarthy throat;
His face unshaven, and none the less,
His hearty laugh and his wholesomeness,
And the wealth of a workman's vote!

Bring him, O Memory, here once more,
And tilt him back in his Windsor chair
By the kitchen-stove, when the day is o'er
And the light of the hearth is across the floor,
And the crickets everywhere!

And let their voices be gladly blent
With a watery jingle of pans and spoons,
And a motherly chirrup of sweet content,
And neighborly gossip and merriment,
And old-time fiddle-tunes!

Tick the clock with a wooden sound,
And fill the hearing with childish glee
Of rhyming riddle, or story found
In the Robinson Crusoe, leather-bound
Old book of the Used-to-be!

John McKeen of the Past! Ah, John,
To have grown ambitious in worldly ways!
To have rolled your shirt-sleeves down, to don
A broadcloth suit, and, forgetful, gone
Out on election days!

John, ah, John! did it prove your worth
To yield you the office you still maintain?
To fill your pockets, but leave the dearth
Of all the happier things on earth
To the hunger of heart and brain?

Under the dusk of your villa trees,
Edging the drives where your blooded span
Paw the pebbles and wait your ease,
Where are the children about your knees,
And the mirth, and the happy man?

The blinds of your mansion are battened to;
Your faded wife is a close recluse;
And your "finished" daughters will doubtless do

Dutifully all that is willed of you,
And marry as you shall choose!

But O for the old-home voices, blent
With the watery jingle of pans and spoons,
And the motherly chirrup of glad content
And neighborly gossip and merriment,
And the old-time fiddle-tunes!

THEIR SWEET SORROW

They meet to say farewell: Their way
Of saying this is hard to say.
He holds her hand an instant, wholly
Distressed and she unclasps it slowly.

He bends his gaze evasively
Over the printed page that she
Recurs to, with a new-moon shoulder
Glimpsed from the lace-mists that enfold her.

The clock, beneath its crystal cup,
Discreetly clicks "Quick! Act! Speak up!"
A tension circles both her slender
Wrists and her raised eyes flash in splendor,

Even as he feels his dazzled own.
Then, blindingly, round either thrown,
They feel a stress of arms that ever
Strain tremblingly and "Never! Never!"

Is whispered brokenly, with half
A sob, like a belated laugh,
While cloyingly their blurred kiss closes,
Sweet as the dew's lip to the rose's.

SOME SCATTERING REMARKS OF BUB'S

Wunst I looked our pepper-box lid
An' cut little pie-dough biscuits, I did,
And cooked 'em on our stove one day
When our hired girl she said I may.

Honey's the goodest thing, Oo-ooh!
And blackberry-pies is goodest, too!
But wite hot biscuits, ist soakin'-wet
Wiv tree-mullasus, is goodest yet!

Miss Maimie she's my Ma's friend, an'

She's purtiest girl in all the lan'!
An' sweetest smile an' voice an' face
An' eyes ist looks like p'serves tas'e'!

I ruther go to the Circus-show;
But, 'cause my parunts told me so,
I ruther go to the Sund'y School,
'Cause there I learn the goldun rule.

Say, Pa, what is the goldun rule
'At's allus at the Sund'y School?

MR. WHAT'S-HIS-NAME

They called him Mr. What's-his-name:
From where he was, or why he came,
Or when, or what he found to do,
Nobody in the city knew.

He lived, it seemed, shut up alone
In a low hovel of his own;
There cooked his meals and made his bed,
Careless of all his neighbors said.

His neighbors, too, said many things
Expressive of grave wonderings,
Since none of them had ever been
Within his doors, or peered therein.

In fact, grown watchful, they became
Assured that Mr. What's-his-name
Was up to something wrong indeed,
Small doubt of it, we all agreed.

At night were heard strange noises there,
When honest people everywhere
Had long retired; and his light
Was often seen to burn all night.

He left his house but seldom then
Would always hurry back again,
As though he feared some stranger's knock,
Finding him gone, might burst the lock.

Beside, he carried, every day,
At the one hour he went away,
A basket, with the contents hid
Beneath its woven willow lid.

And so we grew to greatly blame

This wary Mr. What's-his-name,
And look on him with such distrust
His actions seemed to sanction just.

But when he died, he died one day
Dropped in the street while on his way
To that old wretched hut of his
You'll think it strange, perhaps it is

But when we lifted him, and past
The threshold of his home at last,
No man of all the crowd but stepped
With reverence, Aye, quailed and wept!

What was it? Just a shriek of pain
I pray to never hear again
A withered woman, old and bowed,
That fell and crawled and cried aloud

And kissed the dead man's matted hair
Lifted his face and kissed him there
Called to him, as she clutched his hand,
In words no one could understand.

Insane? Yes. Well, we, searching, found
An unsigned letter, in a round
Free hand, within the dead man's breast:
"Look to my mother, I'm at rest.

You'll find my money safely hid
Under the lining of the lid
Of my work-basket. It is hers,
And God will bless her ministers!"

And some day, though he died unknown
If through the City by the Throne
I walk, all cleansed of earthly shame,
I'll ask for Mr. What's-his-name.

WHEN AGE COMES ON

When Age comes on!
"The deepening dusk is where the dawn
Once glittered splendid, and the dew
In honey-drips, from red rose-lips
Was kissed away by me and you.
And now across the frosty lawn
Black foot-prints trail, and Age comes on
And Age comes on!
And biting wild-winds whistle through

Our tattered hopes and Age comes on!

When Age comes on!
O tide of raptures, long withdrawn,
Flow back in summer-floods, and fling
Here at our feet our childhood sweet,
And all the songs we used to sing! . . .
Old loves, old friends, all dead and gone
Our old faith lost and Age comes on
And Age comes on!
Poor hearts! have we not anything
But longings left when Age comes on?

ENVOY

Just as of old! The world rolls on and on;
The day dies into night, night into dawn
Dawn into dusk through centuries untold.
Just as of old.

Time loiters not. The river ever flows,
Its brink or white with blossoms or with snows;
Its tide or warm with Spring or Winter cold:
Just as of old.

Lo! where is the beginning, where the end
Of living, loving, longing? Listen, friend!
God answers with a silence of pure gold
Just as of old.

James Whitcomb Riley – A Short Biography

Poet and author James Whitcomb Riley was born on October 7th 1849 in Greenfield, Indiana. Known as the "Hoosier Poet" for his work with regional dialects, and as the "Children's Poet" for his children's poetry and devotion to youth causes, Riley is best remembered as the author of the well-loved verse book, *Rhymes of Childhood*.

Riley grew up in a well-off and influential family. Riley's father, Reuben Andrew Riley, was a lawyer and Democrat member of the Indiana House of Representatives and he named his son for his friend James Whitcomb, then the governor of Indiana.

Riley had a spotty education, learning at home and attending his local school sporadically (he did not graduate Grade 8 until the age of twenty). Nonetheless, his was a childhood full of creativity. He learned about poetry from an uncle who was a poet and enthusiast and was encouraged by his mother to write and produce juvenile theatrical presentations. His father taught him how to play the guitar and Riley went on to perform in a local band.

Life changed when Riley's father went off to fight in the Civil War in 1861. The family (which already included six children) took in an additional orphan child and suffered many hardships. Riley would base his famous poem, *Little Orphant Annie* on this temporary foster sibling (both the child and the poem were named "Allie", but a typesetter made a crucial typo when the poem was finally published).

Riley Senior returned from soldiering a broken man, partially paralyzed and unable to resume his practice. The family was forced to sell their house in town and retreated to the family farm where Riley's mother died in 1870. Riley became estranged from his father at this time and left home. He also started drinking excessively, beginning a life-long habit that would both impact his health and his career.

He embarked on a series of low-paying jobs – house painting, Bible salesman – before starting a sign-painting business in Greenfield. Riley wrote catchy slogans for his signs, in effect, his first published verses. He also started participating in local theatre productions and sending poems to the *Indianapolis Mirror* under the pseudonym "Jay Whit".

When he went to work for the McGrillus Company in Anderson, Indiana shilling tonic medicines in a travelling show that visited small towns around the state, he discovered another calling. Riley both wrote and performed skits promoting the tonics. Eventually, Riley and several friends started a billboard company that became successful enough that he was able to turn to writing in a more committed way, and he returned to Greenfield to do so.

Riley started sending out dozens of poems to newspapers around the country and many of them – the *Danbury News*, the *Indianapolis Journal* and the *Anderson Democrat*, among them – published the verses. At the same time, Riley began to write to prominent American writers, sending poems and requesting their endorsement. He was successful with poet Henry Wadsworth Longfellow who wrote back, "I have read the poems with great pleasure, and I think they show a true poetic faculty and insight." Riley would finally meet Longfellow in person shortly before the latter's death in 1882; he famously wrote about the experience and about Longfellow's profound impact on his work.

The *Anderson Democrat* offered Riley a reporting job in 1877. He took it on while continuing to submit poems at journals and newspapers all over the country. Riley would lose the stability of this reporting job when a prank in which he submitted a poem to a journal claiming it was Edgar Allan Poe's went awry. Spurned by many publishers after this embarrassing incident, Riley joined a travelling lecture circuit and gave poetry readings around the state. A born entertainer, Riley's readings would become hugely popular and remained a primary source of income for most of his life.

Eventually, the Poe debacle faded into the background and the *Indianapolis Journal* relented, hiring Riley as a columnist in 1879; he wrote regularly for them about society affairs while continuing to tour his increasingly theatrical and comedic poetry readings. As his fame increased, Riley dropped his "Jay Whit" pseudonym and wrote under his own name from about 1881.

Around this time Riley began writing what are known as his "Boone County poems". They are almost entirely written in dialect and emphasize rural and agricultural topics, often evoking nostalgia for the simplicity of country life. *The Old Swimmin'-Hole* and *When the Frost Is on the Punkin'* were the most popular, and helped earn the entire series critical acclaim. In 1883, a friend arranged for the private publication of *The Old Swimmin' Hole and 'Leven More Poems'*. The book's popularity dictated a second printing before the end of the year and it continued to sell for years, bolstered by Riley's reading tours.

Riley's prose style lent itself well to public performance. With their emphasis on the natural speech rhythms of mid-western dialects, his most famous poems – *Raggedy Man, Little Orphant Annie* – can look slightly ridiculous on the page. But they come alive when read aloud:

Little Orphant Annie's come to our house to stay,
An' wash the cups an' saucers up, an' brush the crumbs away,
An' shoo the chickens off the porch, an' dust the hearth, an'sweep,
An' make the fire, an' bake the bread, an' earn her board-an'-keep;
An' all us other childern, when the supper-things is done,
We set around the kitchen fire an' has the mostest fun
A-list'nin' to the witch-tales 'at Annie tells about,
An' the Gobble-uns 'at gits you
Ef you
Don't
Watch
Out!

This phenomenon is likely the key to Riley's success with children's verse, as well as the reason he was able to build such fame and fortune on the travelling lecture circuit. It helped also that he was a confident and talented performer.

In 1881 Riley was invited to tour with the Redpath Lyceum Circuit, a prominent series that included writers such as Ralph Waldo Emerson on its roster of regular lecturers. After a successful first season reading in Chicago and Indianapolis, Riley signed a ten-year contract with the Circuit and embarked on a tour of the Eastern seaboard starting in Boston. Riley toured with the Circuit until 1885 when he joined forces with humourist Edgar Wilson Nye. In 1888, the pair co-wrote *Nye and Riley's Railway Guide*, a collection of poems and anecdotes. Nye and Riley also teamed up with another famous American humourist Samuel Clemons (Mark Twain) for joint performances in New York City. Despite contract and agent woes that deprived Riley of his full share of the proceeds, he continued touring with Nye through 1890.

Riley published his third compilation of work in 1888. *Old-Fashioned Roses* was written specifically for the British market and consisted mostly of sonnets; Riley intentionally left his country bumpkin dialects out of this collection. The book was a predictable success in the UK and Riley travelled to Scotland (where he made a pilgrimage to the grave of Robert Burns, a poet with who he is often compared) and England to promote it and conduct readings in 1891.

Back home the next year Riley resumed his lecture and reading tour, teaming up with millionaire author Douglass Sherley for a hugely successful double bill. Coinciding with this, in a savvy and astute cross-promotion, Riley compiled and published perhaps his best-loved book, *Rhymes of Childhood*. It's a work that continues to be popular into the 21st century. It also parted the beginning of the end for Riley's literary reputation. Although he continued to sell out readings in New York and across the US (in fact prospective audience members were often turned away), critics increasingly found his work repetitive and banal. His 1894 verse volume *Armazindy* was very poorly received.

Riley gave his last tour in 1895 and spent his final years in Indianapolis writing patriotic poetry for public recitation on civic occasions (with stirring titles such as *America!* and *The Name of Old Glory*) and poem/elegies for famous friends. His life's work of essays, poems, plays and articles was published in sixteen volumes in 1914.

By this time, Riley was in poor health, weakened by years of heavy drinking. The Hoosier Poet died on July 23, 1916 of a stroke. In a final, unusual tribute, Riley lay in state for a day in the Indiana Statehouse, where thousands came to pay their respects. Not since Lincoln had a public personage received such a send-off. He is buried at Crown Hill Cemetery in Indianapolis.

Riley's legacy is not just a literary one. A wealthy man, he left behind the funding seeds for a number of memorial projects, the James Whitcomb Riley Hospital for Children, Camp Riley for children with disabilities and James Whitcomb Riley House (a museum in which the writer's personal effects and furnishings from his lifetime remain unchanged).

And, as a lasting tribute, the town of Greenfield holds a festival every year in Riley's honor. Every October the "Riley Days" festival opens with a flower parade in which local school children place flowers around the statue of Riley set on the courthouse lawn.

Remembered as both a philanthropist and a poet laureate for the Hoosier state of Indiana, a writer with a distinctive pre-industrial folk ethos and an ear for the humble rhythms of the plain local dialect of the US Midwest, Riley remains to this day a poet of the people.

www.ingramcontent.com/pod-product-compliance
Lightning Source LLC
Chambersburg PA
CBHW071309040426
42444CB00009B/1945